T3-BSE-826

The European Bank for Reconstruction and Development

MANCHESTER
UNIVERSITY PRESS

The European Bank for Reconstruction and Development

The building of a bank for East Central Europe

Adam Bronstone

Manchester University Press
Manchester and New York
distributed exclusively in the USA by St. Martin's Press

332.1530947
B86e

Copyright © Adam Bronstone 1999

The right of Adam Bronstone to be identified as the author of this work has been
asserted by him in accordance with the Copyright, Designs and Patents Act 1988.

Published by Manchester University Press
Oxford Road, Manchester M13 9NR, UK
and Room 400, 175 Fifth Avenue, New York, NY 10010, USA
http://www.man.ac.uk/mup

Distributed exclusively in the USA by
St. Martin's Press, Inc., 175 Fifth Avenue, New York,
NY 10010, USA

Distributed exclusively in Canada by
UBC Press, University of British Columbia, 6344 Memorial Road,
Vancouver, BC, Canada V6T 1Z2

British Library Cataloguing-in-Publication Data
A catalogue record for this book is available from the British Library

Library of Congress Cataloging-in-Publication Data applied for

ISBN 0 7190 5551 2   *hardback*

First published 1999

06 05 04 03 02 01 00 99   10 9 8 7 6 5 4 3 2 1

Typeset by Ralph Footring, Derby K H
Printed in Great Britain by Bookcraft (Bath) Ltd, Midsomer Norton

Contents

University Libraries
Carnegie Mellon University
Pittsburgh, PA 15213-3890

v

Acknowledgements and dedication

I want to thank Manchester University Press, and especially Nicola Viinikka, and its anonymous reviewers for their assistance and encouraging comments with respect to the manuscript of this book. I would also like to express my gratitude to the many people at the European Bank for Reconstruction and Development who allowed me to interview them, who gave me access to the documents that I required, and who allowed me to take from the EBRD classified material that was instrumental to this project. I would also like to thank the Canadian officials at the Bank who were helpful in allowing me to attend its annual general meetings.

Finally, I would like to dedicate this work to the people at the EBRD and other like organizations, and those in Central and Eastern Europe who are working to transform this area of the world with, but in many instances without, the visionary assistance of the states of the Western world. Their task is onerous and difficult, but the long-term rewards are enormous and vital to the stability of the whole of Europe.

Abbreviations

CEECs	Central and Eastern European countries
CIS	Commonwealth of Independent States
CMEA	Council for Mutual Economic Assistance
EBRD	European Bank for Reconstruction and Development
EC	European Community
ECO	Economic Co-financing Operation
ECSC	European Coal and Steel Community
ECU	European Currency Unit
EEC	European Economic Community
EFTA	European Free Trade Association
EIB	European Investment Bank
EPU	European Payments Union
ERP	European Recovery Program
EU	European Union
FT	*Financial Times*
G-7	Group of Seven (economic association)
G-24	Group of Twenty-Four
GATT	General Agreement on Tariffs and Trade
GNP	gross national product
IBRD	International Bank for Reconstruction and Development
IFC	International Finance Corporation
IMF	International Monetary Fund

NATO	North Atlantic Treaty Organization
NYT	*New York Times*
OECD	Organization for Economic Cooperation and Development
OEEC	Organization for European Economic Cooperation
PHARE	Poland/Hungary Aid for Reconstruction Enterprise

1

Studying the transformation of
Central Europe: the role of the EBRD

Introduction

The European Bank for Reconstruction and Development (EBRD) was proposed and established within a period of eighteen months. The negotiations concerning its establishment between the member-states were replete with controversy, but were nevertheless completed quickly. This may have been so that the EBRD could begin assisting Central and Eastern European countries (CEECs) in their transition from Communism to capitalism. But were the costs of this decision to negotiate in haste too high? Were issues that demanded greater examination compromised for the sake of acting quickly? If so, then did these issues recur during the day-to-day operation of the EBRD?

A number of works have been published with respect to the origins and legal aspects of the EBRD.[1] All provide an excellent description of its foundations, the context in which it was created and how it evolved through a series of negotiation sessions between officials from the EBRD's founding member-states. However, these publications do not go on to analyse what they, and officials from the EBRD, have identified as the fundamental and controversial issues that have guided the EBRD since its inception.

This book will ask whether or not ideas were important in the disagreement concerning the lending policies of the EBRD during its initial years of operation.[2] The section below will examine the organizational paradigm that has been used to explain the creation and operation of the EBRD. The context in which the EBRD was created is the subject of chapter 3, which will also elucidate how some of the key lending policy-related issues were dealt with during and after the initial negotiating sessions. Subsequent chapters will return to the discussion of organizational paradigms and assess the validity of the initial paradigm, as well as the strengths of alternative paradigms, and the organizational and institutional lessons that can be learned from the EBRD's experience.

Simply put, there is something more practical and less academic that we are searching for. Not only are there theoretical questions at stake in this project, but also those that concern the future direction of the EBRD and the impact that these decisions will have on a range of in-need CEECs.

Thinking about institutions

Prior to an analysis of the work of the EBRD, a brief examination of the theoretical aspects of institution building must be conducted. With respect to organizational theories and the EBRD, Steven Weber is of great value. He examines the reasons why certain institutions are formed as opposed to others and, once agreed to, how these organizations are shaped during negotiations. Weber cites Oran Young's differentiation between power-oriented and utilitarian models. As to the former, certain institutions are established because they reflect the interests of the dominant nation-states of the time and, in some instances, the dominant nation-state. The question then is how do these institutions maintain themselves after the hegemonic decline of the dominant state that is most associated with a given organization? Regime analysis assists, in part, in answering this query. Utilitarian models of institution building may involve rational actors who realize their own benefit will be attained through the creation of a given institution. Young attaches the notion of 'institutional bargaining' to this model to account for the lack of perfect knowledge on the part of the actors, the presence of non-state actors and uncertainty.[3]

However, Weber believes that neither of these international relations models of institution building can account for the creation of the EBRD. Instead, Weber posits that the relationship between the institution and its environment influences its origins, as well as its evolution. In this respect institutions are not judged by their efficiency, but by the 'appropriateness of their form'.[4] The concept of legitimacy is central to determine which institutions are appropriate in a given situation.

In the wake of the collapse of the Soviet empire in 1989, it was deemed appropriate by the member-states of the European Community (EC), notably France, to establish a new organization that would have as its primary objective the transition of Central and Eastern Europe from centrally planned economic systems to those of a capitalist variant. Consequently, instead of being a product of a 'power play' between various nation-states, the EBRD was born of and in an institutional environment in which the majority of Western-styled nation-states had already agreed to a set of ideas, beliefs, goals and objectives. Therefore, while the EBRD is not directly linked to the activities of international organizations such as the International Monetary Fund (IMF), the General Agreement on Tariffs and Trade (GATT) or the World Bank, it is because the member-states of these other institutions had an agreed set of beliefs that the EBRD could be established as quickly as it was.[5] It was because of these agreed ideas concerning economic development and the role of the state in post-socialist economies that the establishment of the EBRD, replacing existing ad hoc multilateral and bilateral agreements, was agreed to by not only the member-states of the EC, but also the United States.

Questions

If Weber's analysis of institution building and the formulation of the EBRD is correct, then one would have expected the negotiations concerning the Bank to have been concluded quickly. Also, when reviewing the EBRD's first two years of operation, one would expect to discover an organization noted for a high level of cooperation, rather than conflict, between the major member-states. But, as this analysis of the EBRD will illustrate, conflict rather than cooperation was the hallmark of EBRD debates on a whole range of issues – issues that should have been solved during the negotiations, or at least without a public airing of such divergences. Consequently, a review of the genesis of the organization, as well as the disputes that have marred its first years, will be conducted first, in chapters 2 and 3. The subsequent chapters will address three organization-related questions:

1   What are the theoretical implications of these divergences?
2   What should have been done differently?
3   Are there lessons to be learned when politicians seek to create new, or remake existing, Western-oriented institutions?

However, given the fact that many of the issues that plagued the EBRD recurred after 1992, when key management changes had already been made, this study will also seek to explore and explain European–US relations at the EBRD in this phase of the institution's existence. Superficial cooperation and underlying disharmony after 1992 will be addressed in chapters 4 and 5, and a related set of questions will be posed in chapter 6.

After this post-1992 phase has been explored, the study will begin to ask theoretical and practical questions with respect to the development of an understanding of these disagreements and disputes. Traditional theories will be examined, as will, if appropriate, alternative paradigms of a more critical and comprehensive nature. It will be asked whether or not this study of European–US relations will be better served by the latter rather than the former. If so, then the study will seek out the possible theoretical and practical implications of this turn to a more critical approach to politics, with a view to understanding cooperation among states as well as the building and maintenance of existing political economic institutions such as the EBRD and the creation of, in the post-Cold War world, new political economic organizations. Finally, a series of concluding remarks will be stated, again related to the theoretical and practical consequences of this study.

Before examining what actually happened with respect to CEECs, it is perhaps useful to set the post-1989 world within an historical context. This context is that of the immediate post-World War Two era. What is interesting about this period are not only the similarities in the problems that faced Europe after 1945 and presently (1989–), but the solutions agreed, at least in the first period. Simply put, could the Western allies have learned from previous experience of building institutions and, if so, what may be the future implications for an institution such as the EBRD? These latter questions will be returned to later, after such a review has been conducted in the next chapter.

The way forward

Questions have been posed and an outline of the proceeding chapters established with respect to the means by which answers may be attained. Along the way, other questions may be noted and followed up. However, the principal aim is to respond directly to the three questions in the section above. By doing so, answers pertaining to both the theoretical and practical implications of EBRD assistance to the CEECs may be ascertained.

The way forward at this juncture is to look back for a moment, rather than forward, and contextualize assistance to Central and Eastern Europe in the 1990s by examining the roles played by a number of institutions and countries in the recovery of Western Europe in the aftermath of World War Two, and the period immediately after the collapse of the Soviet system in the late 1980s. Only then will one be able to begin an in-depth examination of key EBRD issues and the theoretical concerns that surround them.

Notes

1 See S. Weber, 'Origins of the European Bank for Reconstruction and Development', *International Organization*, Vol. 48, No. 1, 1994; P. Menkveld, *Origin and role of the European Bank for Reconstruction and Development*, London: Graham and Trotman, 1992; I. Shihata, *The European Bank for Reconstruction and Development*, London: Graham and Trotman, 1990. For general works on Central and Eastern Europe see J. Pinder, *The European Community and Eastern Europe*, London: Royal Institute of International Affairs, 1991; J. M. C. Rollo, *The new Eastern Europe*, London: Royal Institute of International Affairs, 1990.

2 Weber, 'Origins of the European Bank', defines 'ideas' in this context as concerning a 'partial consensus about the relationship between the state, democracy and market economies, part of a historically and geographically specific stream of ideas about the shape and character of a future Europe and its relations with the rest of the world' (p. 2).

3 *Ibid.*, pp. 3–4.

4 *Ibid.*, p. 5.

5 *Ibid.*, pp. 6–7 and 33.

2

The world before, and after, 1989

Introduction

As mentioned in chapter 1, an understanding of the role of the EBRD in the political and economic transformation of Central and Eastern Europe must be preceded by two specific and related contexts. The first is the assistance given to Western Europe by the United States after World War Two, whereas the second is the aid programmes set up for the CEECs in the wake of the collapse of the Soviet Union and its satellite system. In both instances strategies were devised and formal and informal institutional processes initiated for the benefit of these countries in need.

Whether or not the programmes of the 1990s were similar to and as beneficial as those of the late 1940s and early 1950s will be assessed in two stages. An initial comment will be made in this chapter. A second such comment will be made in the concluding chapter (chapter 6) as part of an evaluation of the strengths and benefits of the EBRD as one of the main institutional arrangements of the post-Cold War period. This will be done because the dominant academic opinion is that the Marshall Plan, broadly conceived, was successful in laying down the conditions that enabled the states of Western Europe to recover, both politically and economically. Whether or nor the same can be said of the

EBRD and its primary benefactors is another question, which is the main topic of discussion at the end of the book.

The Marshall Plan revisited

World War Two had ravaged the entire European continent in political and economic terms. While the former is obvious, the latter, to the casual observer, may be less so. A number of scholarly works on the state of the post-war European economy, and specifically the Western European economy, have been written.[1]

While the years 1945–6 were ones of industrial productivity for Western Europe, this part of the continent still suffered from many difficulties, even given the various US-led programmes already under way. These programmes included: a specific package to the United Kingdom; the still continuing Lend–Lease (although this was to end shortly); the United Nations Relief and Rehabilitation Administration; and loans via the US Export–Import Bank, which amounted to billions of US dollars.[2] These programmes, it should be noted, did not include the occupation zones of the former German state. In the latter, the US administration was attempting to restore coal production in the Ruhr and a process by which Germany would not suffocate under the reparations agreements, as was the case after World War One. If nothing else, the world was trying in the immediate post-war period to right the wrongs of past generations and wars.

But 1947 came with no bright demonstrations of European recovery, or at least no signs of increased recovery that would reach pre-war production levels. Causes of this slowness were multiple. They included: a lack of adequate capital, equipment and plant facilities; a shortage both of workers, because of the casualties of World War Two, and of basic resources such as coal, steel and food; inflation, which was rampant and which prevented people from making purchases with their small wages; the depletion of gold resources; the distortion of trade patterns; and large debt payments, which prohibited resources from being spent on what was required for recovery.[3] All of the above were combined with a severe winter in 1946–7 that did nothing but exacerbate these problems, if not wiping out some of the small economic gains already made throughout the Western part of the continent. Agricultural production was only 83 per cent, industrial output 88 per cent and exports a mere 59 per cent of their 1938 levels. As Hogan states, 'these figures added up to a widespread fatigue and a pervasive sense of pessimism' throughout the continent and in the United States.[4]

This depiction of the state of Western Europe is underlined by the belief held by the US administration that the recovery of Europe in political and economic terms was essential to the interests of the United States. From strategic, political, ideological and economic standpoints, much was to be gained or lost in Europe in the immediate post-war period. As such, a more systematic rather than piecemeal approach to European recovery was needed for the balance to be swung in favour of the United States, rather than its political, strategic, ideological and economic post-war adversary, the Soviet Union. The ideological confrontation, as is seen in Gaddis' *Strategies of containment*, through the writings of George Kennan and his staff at the Policy Planning unit of the US Department of State during and after World War Two, was no less a concern than any of the other issues being discussed at that time, such as hunger and industrial dislocation.[5]

Into the breach stepped the idea of a large infusion of cash by the United States into the European economy. The Hoover report, an investigation undertaken by the former US President, gave credence to a bias towards a German, rather than a balanced Europe-wide, recovery programme. While eventually not executed, owing to disagreement among the various branches of the government, further (implemented) programmes were formed from the ashes of this report. The European Recovery Program (ERP), or the Marshall Plan as it is commonly referred to, was the ultimate product of these ashes.

The Marshall Plan, as initially conceived, was to involve a sum of $6–7 billion, which would be accessible to all European governments and directed by the Europeans themselves.[6] Hogan states that the principal goals of the Plan were to avert economic, social and political chaos in Europe, contain Communism, prevent the collapse of the US export trade and achieve multilateralism in the world (i.e. Western) economy. The only point that one may differ on is that of the goal of containing Communism. The Plan, as it was presented, was to be open to every European state – Eastern and Western alike – without prejudice with regard to the ideological leanings of any country applying for funds. However, the truth may be more that while the United States wanted to appear non-partisan, many in the administration and in the French and English governments did not believe that Stalin, via his Foreign Minister, Molotov, would acquiesce to US economic and monetary demands.[7]

General George Marshall, the then Secretary of State for the United States, unveiled the ERP in a speech at Harvard University on 5 October 1947, in which he said:

> [The Plan should be directed] not against any country or doctrine but against hunger, poverty, desperation, and chaos. Its purpose should be the revival of a working economy in the world so as to permit the emergence of political and social conditions in which free institutions can exist…. any government that is willing to assist in the task of recovery will find full cooperation, I am sure, on the part of the United States Government. Any government which maneuvres to block the recovery of other countries cannot expect help from us…. it would be neither fitting nor efficacious for this Government to

undertake to draw up unilaterally a program designed to place Europe on its feet economically. This is the business of the Europeans. The initiative … must come from Europe … the program should be a joint one, agreed to by a number of, if not all, European nations.[8]

The money was to be there for the Europeans while the door to cooperation with the Soviets was left ajar, ready for the latter to open it and step forward and accept the US gesture of assistance. However, at the Paris conference in late June 1947 between the French, British, Americans and Soviets, Molotov was obstinate in his refusal to subject Soviet economic plans to US scrutiny. Hogan asserts that Bevin, the British Foreign Secretary, believed Molotov's wants were akin to asking the US to write a blank cheque for all of Europe and then go off and not disturb them.[9] Molotov subsequently withdrew from the conference and stated that the US policies would 'divide rather than unify the Continent'.[10]

Robert Marjolin, the first Secretary-General of the Organization for European Economic Cooperation (OEEC), recalled in his memoirs that while the French and British leaders invited the Soviet leadership to participate in the OEEC and in the ERP through Marshall Plan funds, the US administration had a different perspective. Furthermore, Soviet officials were adamant in their objection to restrictive conditions if they accepted funds from the ERP and therefore left the main preparatory conference as well as the ERP itself.[11] The author concedes that there was an unfortunate degree of relief at that juncture, for the French and British delegations believed that it would have been almost impossible for the US Congress to approve an aid package for a country that was perceived as hostile to the United States and its capitalism and democratic traditions.[12]

Thus the Marshall Plan became of one many issues of divisiveness between the United States and the Soviet Union. It was not, however, intended to produce similar results in the Western part of Europe. The talks in 1947 and 1948 were primarily restricted to economic cooperation between the European countries in need, but nonetheless the intention of the United States was to produce some degree of political unity as well. The Versailles Treaty and other institutions established after World War One, such as the League of Nations, were viewed as failures that had assisted in creating the conditions for the rise of the Nazi Party and the onset of World War Two. History was not to be repeated, and therefore the leadership of the United States was intent on securing a strong Europe through a network of regional and international institutional arrangements. Thus the Marshall Plan was a beginning, rather than an end in itself.

For the United States to assist these countries efficiently, a number of organizational initiatives were required and duly established. In July 1947, France and Britain invited twenty-two countries to form the Committee of European Economic Co-operation. Its task was to respond to the Marshall Plan on behalf of all the countries in need and to devise an action plan with respect to the goals and needs of the four-year ERP. After the initial start of this Committee, President Truman responded in kind with the establishment of the Economic Cooperation Act of 1948. This formalized the Marshall Plan by stipulating the amount of financial assistance that would be available and the apparatus that would administer the ERP. The Economic Co-operation Administration was established, with the intention of both administering and supervising the aid programme.[13] Some of its powers included: the chartering of US vessels, on demand, for ERP assistance; the purchasing of commodities; and the termination of aid to any country that did not act in accordance with the goals and mandate of the ERP. Simultaneously, each country involved in the Committee of European Economic Cooperation was informed of a set of criteria by which the ERP would be administered. Any deviance from these criteria could result in the termination of aid. It must be noted, nonetheless, that this set of criteria was intended as a guideline, with primary importance being placed upon the need for economic cooperation between national governments. It was the role of the Economic Cooperation Administration to ensure that such cooperation was taking place. If not, the United States reserved the right to alter ERP proposals and aid disbursements.[14]

Nonetheless, for cooperation among the European countries to occur, a more formalized organization was require than that of the Committee of European Economic Cooperation. In its place, the OEEC was established in April 1948. It was to be the European counterpart to the Economic Cooperation Administration. Rather than sixteen countries talking simultaneously, one body would talk to another, thereby streamlining the aid process. The goal of the OEEC was the 'achievement of a sound European economy through the economic co-operation of its members'.[15] In order to accomplish this, the OEEC was required to submit to the Economic Cooperation Administration (its funding body) a recommended list of programmes and financial assistance for each country in need.[16]

This process was not without its difficulties. ERP organizations were fraught with differences of opinion between the United States and its Western European partners. France and Britain perceived the United States as domineering, and both governments worked closely to ensure that both the composition of the executive committee and the details of the constitution of the ERP were minimalist in representation, European in bias and nation-state centric in approach.[17] Because of these differences, Milward concludes that the Marshall Plan/ERP was a failure insofar as it was unable to achieve a number of its initial goals, namely the political reconstruction and integration of Western Europe. However, it could also be said that while the ERP itself was ineffective, it did provide a forum for concerns that would lay the groundwork for other important economic programmes, namely the European Payments Union (EPU). One example of this was the Plan of Action. Submitted by the Consultative Group, the Plan concerned long-term issues such as the need for an increase in exports, the expansion of intra-European trade, concerted investment programmes and financial and monetary stabilization.[18] While Milward considers the Plan an ill-conceived amalgam of US and European interests, it is worth noting that the related issues of trade and currency convertibility were to prove important in the very near future.

Because of the importance of foreign trade with respect to the prosperity of a country, the lack of intra-European trade became, by the late 1940s, a key concern. Given the demands of the time, the creation of the IMF and GATT at Bretton Woods in 1945 had not yet proved helpful. Western Europe was not yet stable enough for the resources of these two organizations to be utilized and, given the bickering that was the hallmark of the Marshall Plan, another means by which stabilization and trade flows could be established and re-established was necessary for the eventual long-term recovery of Western Europe. One result of this need was the US proposal for a small and regulated customs union, which came on the heels of similar thinking already under way in France and Italy, with the UK deciding to opt out of such a venture, along with the Scandinavian countries and the Netherlands. A Franco-Italian union was then mooted but, because of its lack of scope, was eventually dropped. Western Europe was forced to go back to the drawing board to find solutions for its economic problems.

When it did, many were found, but few gained general acceptance. Belgium supported the idea of a European Bank, modelled on the US Federal Reserve, and the United Kingdom, given the strength of the sterling zone, suggested the eventual creation of a larger sterling zone throughout Western Europe.[19] Both were rejected for obvious reasons: no country was prepared, politically or economically, to devolve its economic and fiscal power to a central bank, and the United States was against the idea of the creation of what would be a rival currency. Last, but certainly not least, it was suggested that Marshall aid should be conditional upon the liberalization of trade.[20] Given the apolitical nature of the latter proposal, it appeared to be the one that not only made the most sense, but also that had the greatest chance of succeeding.

In order for intra-European trade to flourish, there had to be the prior stabilization of the balance of payments of these same Western European countries and a move to currency convertibility beyond that of sterling. Washington was in favour of these proposals and was willing provide financial support, as long as the move to trade liberalization was considerable and, unlike a proposal from the United Kingdom, did not produce tariff reductions on important items such as foodstuffs and manufactured items.[21] In turn, the move to a payments union would allow not only intra-European trade to grow, but also a prosperity and stability that would render the IMF, World Bank and GATT useful for the first time since all three had been established.

On 19 September 1950, the EPU came into existence. It was not, however, to be the move towards European integration that the United States desired, because of its economic limitations, but neither did it allow the United Kingdom to enlarge its own currency zone eastwards. On its own terms, the EPU operated as it should have: as a smaller version of the IMF, with the financial support of the United States, and encouraging and discouraging certain patterns of behaviour by its Western European members. For example, trade liberalization on a multilateral rather than bilateral manner was encouraged, while balance-of-payments deficits were not.[22] Two years later, the success of the EPU can be seen by the difficulties the US government had with respect to the continuation of funds for it. Treasury Secretary Snyder commented that while the dollar problem had been solved, there may 'be a day before too long when we may be concerned about its position in world trade, and we do not want to build up an organization that would place us at a complete disadvantage'.[23] Western Europe had gone from being perceived as economically devastated to a continent of states that might become an economic rival, the surest sign that the EPU, and the stability and trade liberalization that followed, was one of the key ingredients to economic recovery.

It must also be mentioned at this juncture that the EPU should not be viewed as an agreement operating in a vacuum, for it was agreed to after Robert Schuman, the French Foreign Minister, had proposed the creation of the European Coal and Steel Community (ECSC). The intention behind the ECSC was to lock forever France and Germany into an economic association that would render war futile. This would be accomplished by taking the materials of war – coal and steel – and placing them under the auspices of a 'high authority' of a supranational organization. By doing so, neither France nor West Germany would be in control of its own assets, making war between the two virtually impossible. Together with Italy and the Benelux countries (Belgium, the Netherlands and Luxembourg), the countries agreed to a union with overtly political intentions that would, in 1958, lead to the establishment of the European Economic Community (EEC). Both organizations would create and help establish a code of conduct, constitutional regulations and patterns of behaviour that would forever alter the way in which these countries related to each other in the realms of the political, economic, military and social. Combined with the creation of the North Atlantic Treaty Organization (NATO) in 1949, the Western part of Europe was marked by an unprecedented degree of institutionalization, which allowed for the recovery of its economies, political systems and the reintegration of both Italy and (West) Germany into the Western political orbit. The EPU in particular can be credited with the success of the latter, insofar as this was the first organization that the leadership of West Germany asked to be included in. In response to the German request, a communiqué following a meeting of the Economic Coordination Administration, the US body overseeing Marshall aid, stated that 'the Ministers considered it appropriate to support and foster the progressive integration of the German people into the European Community'.[24] The subsequent creation of the ECSC brought some concerns on the part of the Economic Cooperation Administration, but overall it concluded that this development was an important step towards trade liberalization and the creation of a competitive market.[25]

Milward is of the opinion that the Marshall Plan was effective in that it assisted in the importation by Western Europe of capital goods. However, in most other respects, it was of less importance than is generally considered by most academics.[26] He adds that this ineffectiveness can be seen by the development of the ECSC, in that it did not fully promote the trade liberalization agenda of the ERP. Instead, it created a cartel for steel and coal producers under heavy government regulation. However, these truths do not discourage one from citing Edmund Hall-Patch's comments shortly after the idea of a customs union was floated. The leader of the British delegation to the Committee of European Economic Cooperation stated that:

> now, as a result of the Marshall proposals, European imaginations have been fired. The financial position of Europe is so desperate that there is a chance, which may never recur, to break down the barriers which are hampering trade revival in Europe.

It may even be possible to go some way towards the integration of the European economy comparable to the vast industrial integration of the United States.[27]

It is not the purpose here to comment on the merits, or otherwise, of the Marshall Plan per se. It is important though to know whether or not the Plan was useful in any way, shape or form because of the similarities that the countries and people of Central and Eastern Europe presently face. Milward makes a strong case for the position that Marshall aid was ineffective and that the strategies that were of the most assistance to the recovery and reconstruction of Western Europe were those of a European nature, namely the EPU and the ECSC. However, it must not be taken for granted that – as much as France, the United Kingdom and other countries disagreed with the tactics and policies of the United States – there was a genuine attempt to shape a different future for Western Europe. And even if Western European states *were* driven to seek out their own future without the assistance of the United States, then Marshall aid and the overall presence of the United States can still be said, as a result of some reaction against it, to have contributed to European recovery and reconstruction. But the question that can be asked is what could the future of Europe have been like had the United States not acted in the unilateral manner that it did, insofar as this created a series of long-running disputes between itself and a number of the key actors (states) of the region? Would an alternative to Marshall aid have been more effective? Would a different, and possibly better, organization than the European Union have been established? Would the United Kingdom have joined the ECSC at its inception in 1952 and likewise the EEC in 1958?

It is not ours to judge and think about history with perfect hindsight. It may be sufficient to state that the Marshall Plan in and of itself was a bold gesture on the part of the United States for a number of self-interested and altruistic reasons. It was conceived in good faith, but became mired in disagreement between one country interested in trade liberalization (the United States) and its partners, which, while not completely against this, were more in favour of regulated arrangements that would assist in the recovery of the European economic system. In subsequent chapters, when the EBRD is analysed and similar issues reappear – the presence of an economically devastated area of Europe, unilateralism on the part of the United States, discord with its Western European allies and an institution mired in disagreement – one must remember the lessons of history and ask not whether more could have been done, for more can always be done, but why it was not done and how these mistakes might be corrected, given the potential implications if such mistakes are left unchecked.

1989 and beyond – new context, old issues

Immediately after the collapse of the Soviet empire, the CEECs were faced with numerous economic and industrial challenges similar to those that faced Western Europe after World War Two. These included: a dramatic decline in industrial output; inflation that reached hyperinflationary levels in some countries; obsolete production facilities; a workforce that is, to a certain extent, unmotivated and must be retrained to think and act in a free market environment rather than one that is centrally planned; and the shadow of political instability.[28]

To assist in the transformation of these economies the Western world established, either bilaterally or multilaterally, through a number of international institutions such as the World Bank's International Bank for Reconstruction and Development (IBRD), the IMF and the EC, a number of aid-related programmes. Trade and cooperative agreements between the EC and Poland and

Hungary resulted in the creation of the Poland/Hungary Aid for Reconstruction Enterprise (PHARE) programme and numerous sums of capital, in the form of grants, aid and trade credits, were extended to CEECs by both the member-states of the EC – in particular France and Germany – and the United States.[29]

However, the EC was more involved in these reconstruction programmes than either the United States or Japan. Germany and France proceeded to establish, both bilaterally and through the mechanisms of the EC, a number of programmes directed to CEECs.[30] Weber notes that the relationship of Japan and the United States with Central and Eastern Europe was one of 'studied detachment', because of their geographical and political distance.[31] Weber comments that the United States found itself constrained in its ability to act in concert with the EC because of its Cold War relationship with Central and Eastern Europe and the Soviet Union. Perceiving the assistance of CEECs as being part of its larger relationship with the Soviet Union, US officials attempted to fashion a balance between their policies towards the Soviet Union and CEECs.[32]

Nonetheless, US officials recognized that the United States had a vital interest in the establishment of democracy and market-based economies in Central and Eastern Europe. A successful transformation of this area of Europe would consolidate the demise of the Soviet empire and assist in binding these states to the Western pillar on the European continent, the EC. Such a transition would assist in the stabilization of these states. A number of US officials also contend that the US interest in seeing the CEECs bound to the EC was part of a larger US–EC project, of which the signing of the Transatlantic Declaration in 1990 was another element. One aspect of this document called on the EC to 'assume a place as a responsible leader contributing to the strengthening of structures of global as well as continental interdependence'.[33] In 1991 Secretary of State James Baker had called on the EC to demonstrate its foreign policy competence by being able to 'reach out to the East'.[34] Also of great importance to the United States was that the promotion of economic reforms and liberalization in formerly socialist countries would allow America to 'champion its economic ideology agenda, stressing free markets, private control, and the removal of state intervention in economies as the path to prosperity'.[35]

It was on the basis of these interests that the member-states of the EC and the United States met in April 1989 to map out a coherent strategy with respect to the transformation of Central and Eastern Europe. At a meeting of the Group of Twenty-Four (G-24), the EC was formally asked to coordinate the Western response to the ongoing transformation of Central and Eastern Europe and the former Soviet Union. The final communiqué of the meeting stated that, because of the events unfolding in Central and Eastern Europe:

> Each of us is prepared to support this process and to consider, as appropriate and in a coordinated fashion, economic assistance aimed at transforming and opening their economies in a desirable manner.... We believe that each of us should direct our assistance to these countries so as to sustain the momentum of reform through inward investment, joint ventures ... and other ventures which would develop a more competitive economy.... To these ends, we ask the Commission of the European Community to take the necessary initiatives in agreement with the other member-states of the Community, and to associate, besides the summit participants, all interested countries.[36]

At this stage, however, the creation of a new institution such as the EBRD was not the only option being considered by the G-24. A number of influential people called instead for the establishment of a policy similar to the Marshall Plan. Wim Duisenberg, then head of the Netherlands' central bank, stated in a journal article that 'a similar form of close cooperation ... on trade and exchange rates – is needed today'.[37] Also, the possibility of using the resources of existing institutions such as the IMF, World Bank and the International Finance Corporation was discussed, as well as the continuation of national, regional and international forms of assistance.[38] The notion of a new institution, with a different set of criteria and objectives from those of these other organizations, was mooted by member-states at this meeting of the Paris Club (an informal subgrouping of the G-24).

Finally, it was a speech by President Mitterrand that spurred on the establishment of the EBRD. In his address to the European Parliament on 26 October 1989, the French leader urged the EC to seize the opportunity given to it by the Paris Club and to initiate new policies that would aid in the transformation of Central and Eastern Europe. Mitterrand said that:

> Poland, Hungary, the Soviet Union and, in his historic leading role, Mr. Gorbachev, need to be helped.... What can Europe do? ... Why not set up a Bank for Europe which, like the European Investment Bank, would finance major projects and have on its Board of Directors the twelve European countries. Not to mention the others, such as Poland and Hungary, and why not the Soviet Union and yet others? ... It was done for technology ... under Eureka, so what is holding us back? Is the area of finance sacrosanct, or is not being an expert or a president or chairman of the board of something a disqualification? The creation of a Bank for Europe is a highly political decision.[39]

Following this address, the member-states of the European Council, meeting on 8–9 December, formally endorsed the concept of a bank with the specific task of aiding the transition of CEECs and the republics of the former Soviet Union. The final declaration of the meeting stated that the Council was:

convinced in the present circumstances that all must, more than ever, demonstrate their sense of responsibility. The changes and transitions which are necessary must not take place to the detriment of the stability of Europe but rather must contribute to strengthening it.... Far from wanting to derive unilateral advantage from the present situation, the Community and its Member States mean to give their support to the countries which have embarked upon the road to democratic change.... The Community and its Member States are fully convinced of the common responsibility which devolves on them in this decisive phase in the history of Europe ... [and has] drawn up conclusions which illustrate this intention.... at this time of profound and rapid change the Community is and must remain a point of reference and influence. It remains the cornerstone of a new European architecture and, in its will to openness, the mooring for a future European equilibrium.[40]

Conclusions

As was the case with Europe in the immediate wake of World War Two, Central and Eastern Europe after the demise of the Soviet empire faced a number of cumulative problems. The question facing Western Europe, and the Western nations as a whole, was whether or not they were prepared to act in a manner befitting the political leadership of the 1940s. Would another George Marshall come to the fore and lead a multinational rebuilding effort? Would the allies be able to act in unison for the benefit of Central and Eastern Europe, as well as themselves? And if so, would it be too little and too late, and be bogged down in recriminations and dissension, or just enough and timely in its intervention?

The next chapter seeks to answer some of these questions. Having set out the need for some kind of coordinated Marshall-styled plan for the countries of Central and Eastern Europe, the primary question is whether the Western allies acted in a

Marshall-type fashion, insofar as their ability to overcome differences allowed, to produce a credible, and useful, solution.

Notes

1 See I. Wexler, *The Marshall Plan revisited*, Westport: Greenwood Press, 1983; and H. Price, *The Marshall Plan and its meaning*, Ithaca: Cornell University Press, 1955.

2 M. Hogan, *The Marshall Plan*, Cambridge: Cambridge University Press, 1987, p. 29.

3 *Ibid.*, p. 30.

4 *Ibid.*

5 *Ibid.*, pp. 26–7. See also J. Gaddis, *Strategies of containment*, New York: Oxford University Press, 1982.

6 Hogan, *Marshall Plan*, p. 42.

7 *Ibid.*, p. 52.

8 Cited in D. Acheson, *Present at the creation*, London: Weidenfield and Nicolson, 1969, pp. 233–4.

9 Hogan, *Marshall Plan*, pp. 51–2.

10 *Ibid.*, p. 52.

11 R. Marjolin, *Architect of European unity*, London: Weidenfeld and Nicolson, 1989, p. 182.

12 *Ibid.*

13 Wexler, *Marshall Plan revisited*, p. 30.

14 *Ibid.*, p. 214.

15 *Ibid.*, p. 208.

16 *Ibid.*

17 A. Milward, *The reconstruction of Western Europe 1945–51*, Los Angeles: University of California Press, 1984, p. 180.

18 *Ibid.*, pp. 203–4. The Consultative Group was a high-level group of Western European politicians that made suggestions concerning what the ERP should do, and how.

19 *Ibid.*, pp. 262 and 278–9.

20 *Ibid.*, p. 281.

21 *Ibid.*, p. 303.

22 *Ibid.*, p. 331.

23 *Ibid.*, p. 334.

24 *Ibid.*, p. 313.

25 *Ibid.*, p. 399; see also p. 474.

26 *Ibid.*, pp. 469–70.

27 *Ibid.*, p. 239.

28 Differences existed between the CEECs. Poland, Hungary, the Czech Republic, Bulgaria and Slovakia are noted as those that are better off than the others. For details see EBRD, *Annual report*, 1991.

29 P. Menkveld, *Origin and role of the European Bank for Reconstruction and Development*, London: Graham and Trotman, 1992, pp. 22–3. For details on PHARE see Appendix A.

30 S. Weber, 'Origins of the European Bank for Reconstruction and Development', *International Organization*, Vol. 48, No. 1, 1994, pp. 12–17. See Appendix B for a selection of EC programmes for Central and Eastern Europe.

31 *Ibid.*, pp. 17–19.

32 *Ibid.*, pp. 19–20.

33 United States Information Service, *Declaration on US–EC relations*, 23 November 1990.

34 J. Baker, 'Opportunities to build a new world order', US Information Services, 6 February 1991.

35 *New York Times* (*NYT*), 13 December 1989, p. 18.

36 Cited by Weber, 'Origins of the European Bank for Reconstruction and Development', p. 21.

37 W. Duisenberg, 'Lessons of the Marshall Plan', *European Affairs*, Vol. 5, No. 3, July 1991, p. 21. Also see comments by Z. Brzezinski, 'For Eastern Europe, a $25 billion aid package', *NYT*, 7 March 1990, p. A25.

38 Weber, 'Origins of the European Bank for Reconstruction and Development', p. 26.

39 European Community, *Official Journal of the European Community*, 25 December 1989, p. 149.

40 European Community, *Bulletin of the European Community*, EC 12–1989, pp. 14–15.

3

Creation and conflict – first-year EBRD blues

Introduction

Chapters 1 and 2 have laid the groundwork with respect to the thesis of the study, its plan of action and questions to be asked. They have also placed the establishment of the EBRD within not one but two important and related contexts – the recovery of Western Europe after World War Two and the state of Central and Eastern Europe after the collapse of the Soviet empire in 1989. This chapter details the negotiations concerning the establishment of the Bank. It documents the charter, principles and operational philosophy of the EBRD, as well as the various disagreements that plagued the institution during and after its founding. Only after the iteration of the various disagreements, and an initial reading of why they occurred, can this study, in the next chapter, begin to make theoretical headway with respect to being able to explain and understand these disagreements.

The founding of the EBRD

The European Council decided that the EBRD would have as its objective the task of promoting 'productive and competitive investment in the states of Central and Eastern Europe ... to assist the transition towards a more market-oriented economy and to speed up the necessary structural adjustments'.[1] To this end, the countries of Western Europe, North America, Asia and the CEECs in need agreed to establish the European Bank. By May 1990, forty states had agreed to the basic principles of the EBRD. These states included all of the member-states of the European Union (EU) – along with the EU itself and the European Investment Bank (EIB, which is an EU institution) themselves – the United States, Japan, Canada and all of the CEECs, along with the then Soviet Union.[2] With respect to voting shares, the countries of the EU, along with the EU and the EIB, control 51 per cent of the shares, while the United States is the single largest shareholder, with a 10 per cent share. Thus the EU, when acting as a block along with the EU representative and the EIB, can pass some decisions without the consent of the United States. This ability is considered by EU officials at the EBRD as a significant aspect of the Bank and has heightened awareness of the role of the EU in aiding Central and Eastern Europe in its transitional period.[3]

However, there are a number of policy-related issues at the EBRD that can be decided only by qualified majority voting of either 75 or 85 per cent of all of the voting members, and the presence of two-thirds or three-quarters of the voting members, depending on the issue. The membership, total amount of capital at the institution, the allotment of shares and the method of operation (a 60/40 per cent division between private and public projects) of the EBRD all require two-thirds of the members to be present and a 75 per cent majority. The use of loans by recipient countries is the only issue that requires the presence of three-quarters of the members and an 85 per cent majority. This latter voting requirement was mentioned in articles 8 and 56 of the Bank's charter, as amended. The result is that the United States, the sponsor of this requirement, along with one other larger shareholding country, can create a 'blocking majority' on this issue. Finally, the initial capitalization of the EBRD was $12 billion, with every shareholder investing its percentage of 'stock' that it owns in the Bank itself. Thus, as a collective, the Western Europeans have contributed to the EBRD roughly $6 billion, while the US share is $1.2 billion.

The goals and purposes of the EBRD are stated in the opening paragraphs of the charter of the institution. The overall purpose is to 'foster the transition towards open market-oriented economies and to promote private and entrepreneurial initiative in the Central and Eastern European countries committed to and applying the principles of multiparty democracy, pluralism and market economies'.[4]

Article 2 of the charter goes on to spell out the eight specific functions of the Bank. These are:

1   the promotion of private sector activity;
2   the mobilization of foreign and domestic capital;
3   the fostering of productive investment in infrastructure;
4   the provision of technical expertise;
5   the stimulation of the development of capital markets;
6   the support of multi-country projects;
7   the support of environmentally conscious projects;
8   any other activity that may further the attainment of the above seven functions.[5]

It was remarkable that an institution of this scope and size was able to move from idea to reality in less than two years; it stands as a testament in itself to the political will of all those leaders involved in the institution and their commitment to the transformation of these states in need and their transition to market economies and democratic traditions throughout society. As such, the EBRD had great expectations placed upon it from the start. A journalist reporting from the signing ceremony of the charter by all the member-states of the Bank remarked that the 'bank is one of the most important international aid projects to be established since World War II'.[6] President Mitterrand was quoted as saying that the EBRD was a step towards the development of a 'great Europe'.[7] The new President of the EBRD, Mr Jacques Attali, a former economic and political advisor to the French President, also was found to be saying that the 'Bank will not be a replication of existing traditional institutions ... it will use different techniques, and act in both the private and public sectors'.[8] He went on to state that the Bank will act as a 'catalyst' and 'door-opener' for others and that the very establishment of the EBRD was 'significant in that it marks the end of the cold war era ... former enemies have been able to sit down at the same table as equals and discuss something other than arms control'.[9]

This perception of the EBRD's role vis-à-vis Central and Eastern Europe by Attali was stressed in the Bank's annual general report of April 1992. In his report, President Attali stated that:

> the Bank has now become an essential instrument in channelling international support [to the East], a catalyst and a partner for the business and banking community. It is a unique institution to deal with a unique situation. Not solely a developmental bank, or a merchant bank ... it is also the only institution entirely devoted to the success of transition both to democracy and to the market economy. For all those involved in this formidable task, it [the EBRD] is becoming a focal point for knowledge, experience and the exchange of ideas.... if the transition succeeds without tragedy or violence, the European Bank, together with other institutions, will have provided an impetus for what the whole of Europe could become – a centre of culture and creativity and a continent of freedom and justice, with a sound economic and physical environment, playing its part in the creation of a more tolerant and peaceful world.[10]

This line taken by Attali fits in very closely with the political aspects of the EBRD's mandate. An EBRD document dedicated to this very issue stated in its foreword that the Board of Directors of the Bank approved of procedures that would implement these 'political' aspects in ways that 'recognize the critical link between the political and economic aspects of the Agreement [the EBRD charter].'[11] These links, which are mentioned in general terms, are stated quite clearly in the preamble to the charter, which states that the contracting parties should be:

> committed to the fundamental principles of multiparty democracy, the rule of law, respect for human rights and market economies ... recalling the Final Act of the Helsinki Conference on Security and Cooperation in Europe, and in particular its Declaration on Principles; ... welcoming the intent of Central and Eastern European countries to further the practical implication of multiparty democracy, strengthening democratic institutions, the rule of law and respect for human rights and their willingness to implement reforms in order to evolve towards market-oriented economies ... [and the parties] ... have agreed to establish hereby the European Bank for Reconstruction and Development.[12]

Article 11 of the EBRD's charter establishes a role for the Board of Directors with respect to ensuring that the principles and goals of the institutions are adhered to in the countries of operation. Section 2(ii) states that in their review the directors should consider progress by the country in 'decentralization, demonopolization and privatization and the relative share of the Bank's lending to private enterprises, to state-owned enterprises in the process of transition to participation in the market-oriented economy'.[13] While 'democratic institutions' are not mentioned in this section of article 11, the Political Unit of the Bank does have a mandate to hold countries of operation to certain 'negative' criteria, under which they can have their borrowing rights terminated. These criteria or benchmarks of fulfilment consist of free elections, an independent judiciary and the guarantee of the freedom of speech, movement, conscience and religion.[14] If any one of the countries that is involved in EBRD-sponsored projects suffers political setbacks, it is therefore incumbent upon the Board, and specifically the President, to decide whether or not such ongoing projects should be halted and further ones suspended until the country in question improves not only its economic progress but its political progress as well.

The negotiations

It is fair to say that US officials, among others, were not wholly agreeable to the idea of creating a new multilateral development bank. Thus the negotiations leading up to the establishment of the EBRD were replete with disagreements over a wide range of issues. In brief, these included the status of the Soviet Union, the potential lack of influence in this institution compared with that which the US commands in the World Bank and IMF, and the historical adversarial nature of the relationship between the Reagan and Bush administrations and developmental banks in Asia, Africa and Latin America. Many of these and other issues that plagued the establishment of the EBRD will be dealt with below.

Non-state actors

The US officials were initially against the inclusion of the EIB as an independent shareholder in the Bank. The EIB is the developmental bank of the EU, wholly owned by the member-states of the EU. It lends capital only to public sector projects. While eventually overruled by senior US negotiators, economic officials were concerned about the perceived 'state socialism' of the EIB. The inclusion of a decidedly pro-public sector institution in an organization that the United States wanted to promote free market capitalism might send the wrong signals to the political and business leaders of the CEECs. One US official involved in the negotiations stated that the activities of the EIB 'may not match the private sector emphasis we are seeking for the bank.'[15]

Public versus private money

From the time of the negotiations concerning the EBRD, the debate about to its exact role and how its principles and guidelines for action and decision making with respect to proposed ventures began. One issue of contention was the amount of capital that was to be allocated for private distribution and that loaned to governments to fund infrastructure projects. The European Council's declaration of support for the EBRD initiative, as quoted publicly in December 1989, stated that the function of the Bank would be to promote 'productive and competitive investment in the States of Central and Eastern Europe'.[16] Menkveld notes that productive and competitive investment need not come from private sector sources alone.[17] There are, as seen by various multilateral regional banks, many public sector sources of competitive and productive investment. Consequently, the prioritization of one form of investment over another was not alluded to in this statement. The same might be said of a statement made by Attali, who was once quoted as saying that there was a need in the CEECs to create 'effective economies' rather than 'market economies'.[18] Again, a lack of prioritization of one kind of investment or economic model may be noted.

However, the delegation representing the United States was of a different opinion. The US administration, along with the government of the United Kingdom, was opposed to funds going to the public rather than the private sector. Any emphasis on the former would be, for these governments, akin to the subsidization of failing or failed state socialism.[19] The two countries insisted on changing the wording from 'productive and competitive' to 'private'.[20] David Mulford, the Assistant Treasury Secretary for International Affairs for the United States and its chief negotiator during the preparatory meetings of the EBRD, was quoted as saying that without this emphasis on the private sector 'the risk was that all loans would go to governments and end up financing the status quo rather than change'.[21] Probably the most important debate immediately before the formal opening of the EBRD had begun.

In hindsight, one staff member of the EBRD has remarked that the debate over private and public sector orientation was an 'obvious dividing line between the Continental Europeans and the Anglo-Saxon countries, as well as the Japanese'.[22] The Europeans, save for the British, were of roughly one mind when it came to the economic orientation of the institution. Similarly, one European official was quoted as saying that Europeans 'view American attitudes toward the public sector as dogmatic. They perceive it as necessarily negative. We [Europeans] agree on promoting private enterprise, but we'd like less rigidity'.[23] One German official supported that belief when he said that the German government, along with the great majority of EC countries, was 'not in favor of having written down a strict division of how financial resources should be invested'.[24] The Americans, on the other hand, were persistent and it is commented by many inside and outside the Bank that the divide between the two positions was somewhat stark. An example of this was when a US senator stated that 'European policy-makers … are indifferent, if not hostile, to growth economies … [and] still think that socialism can be reformed'.[25]

In the end, the US position prevailed – a majority of the Bank's capital had to be earmarked for private as opposed to public sector investment. The Europeans, on the other hand, did not press for any specific figure or division of emphasis between the merchant and development banking divisions of the organization, with their respective orientations to private and public projects. The German officials were of the belief that this was a policy that should have been allowed to 'develop over time'.[26] But almost regardless of this, the Americans received what they had pressed for. The Bank's mandate, as detailed in article 11.3 (i) and (ii) of the charter, states that:

> not more than forty (40) per cent of the amount of the Bank's total committed loans, guarantees and equity investments ... shall be provided to the state sector. Such percentage limit shall apply initially over a two (2) year period, from the date of commencement of the Bank's operations ... and thereafter of each subsequent financial year.... for any country, not more than forty (40) per cent of the Bank's total committed loans, guarantees and equity investments over a period of five (5) years ... shall be provided to the state sector.[27]

The 'state sector' was defined as being that part of the economy of a country that includes 'national and local Governments, their agencies, and enterprises owned or controlled by any of them'.[28] No definition of what 'owned or controlled' was given at the time of the commencement of the Bank's operations, nor of the term 'private sector'. With respect to the latter, 60 per cent of all of the Bank's capitalization was to be allocated to such programmes. Ronald Freedman, the head of European investment banking at Salamon Brothers, one of the top Wall Street brokerage firms, was selected as the First Vice-President of the EBRD, in charge of the merchant banking division.

Soviet status, or old enemies die hard

A third major dispute concerned the status of the Soviet Union and whether or not it should be allowed to become a member of the institution. Even if membership were allowed, the amount of capital that the Soviet Union could borrow from the EBRD was disputed. In his speech to the European Parliament, Mitterrand had suggested that the Soviet Union, along with Poland, Hungary and other CEECs, should be included in the membership of his proposed European bank.[29] The rest of the Twelve, while possibly more cautious than the French with respect to this issue, were of a similar opinion. The Americans, as was the case in 1947 with regard to the ERP, were adamant in their objection to Soviet membership of the organization. President Bush was quoted as stating that one of his main reasons for objecting to the Soviet Union as a member was that the founding reason for the Bank from the perspective of the United States was to 'help the smaller countries in Eastern Europe who are going down democracy's road'.[30] Thus the status of the Soviet Union as a full participant with lending rights was in doubt. The Americans pressed for 'observer status' while the Europeans, including the British, stood as one and wanted the Soviet Union to have full membership, with the same lending rights as all the other CEECs. This would mean that there would have been no lending restrictions placed upon the Soviets, save for those that applied to all recipient countries.

The EC countries were 'victorious' in that the Soviet Union was granted full membership, but had to accept a compromise on the subject of lending capabilities. For the Americans, the status of the Soviet Union was fast becoming what one EBRD employee has called a 'participation' issue.[31] Had the Soviet been granted full lending rights, as was the case with the CEECs, the US government was ready to withdraw its support for the Bank.[32]

Nicholas Brady, the American Secretary of the Treasury and representative to the EBRD, lent even further weight to Bush's remarks by saying that 'our position is we would not be prepared to join [the EBRD] if the Soviet Union had borrowing powers beyond their share of capital'.[33] As such, a settlement that would allow the Americans to continue in the EBRD negotiations was reached, albeit reluctantly on the part of the Western Europeans. This was that the Soviet Union would be allowed to borrow 30 per cent of its total share in the EBRD, which equalled the paid-in share of its total subscription. This restriction meant that the Soviets were confined to lending a sum total of 2 per cent of the Bank's funds, for its total shareholding in the EBRD was 6 per cent, and even that figure was decided through a compromise between the EC countries and the United States.

Related to the above arguments concerning the status of the Soviet Union was also the amount of stock it could hold in the EBRD. A proposal was 'floated' to all the potential major shareholders of the EBRD that the United States, France, the United Kingdom, Germany and Japan should receive an equal amount of shares in the institution while the EC states, along with the EC itself and the EIB, would control an overall majority of the stock. All the EC states stressed their desire for a combined majority of the voting shares, for this would emphasize the 'European' character of the Bank.[34] However, the Soviet Union's share of stock in the EBRD as proposed was unacceptable to the United States, as was the US percentage of the total shares. In the end, the United States received and paid for 10 per cent, the Soviet Union only 6 and Japan 8.5 per cent; the member-states of the EC together with the EC itself and the EIB controlled more than 51 per cent of the total stock, with France, Germany, Italy and the United Kingdom holding the largest amounts at 8.5 per cent each.[35] The Europeans therefore began with a working majority, but the Americans were the single largest shareholder and the Soviets were confined to a third tier, with less than all of the above countries but more than the CEECs (see Appendix C).

By 17 June 1991, Attali was calling on the EBRD's Board of Governors to ease the restrictions placed upon the Bank with respect to the percentage of capital it was allowed to lend to the Soviet Union. This call came after a meeting at the Bank's headquarters between Attali and President Gorbachev. The former, in a press statement, said that while there were many economic and political decisions to be taken regarding the conversion of the rouble, laws on property, enterprises and the means of creating private enterprises, and relations between the centre and the republics, he still found Gorbachev 'fully committed to reforms'.[36] This meeting between the two men was also an attempt to secure for Gorbachev an invitation to the upcoming Group of Seven (G-7) summit.[37] Attali, at the same press conference, also stated, in a veiled gesture to the US administration, that this decision with respect to the capital allowances to the Soviet Union could be 'taken at any time by the board ... in order to improve the capacity of the bank to act ... [and] we [in the Bank] can only welcome any green light to go more quickly in terms of financing privatisation and reforms [in the Soviet Union]'.[38]

These plans for privatisation and reform of the Soviet economy, which Attali had referred to as necessary and thus requiring a change to the EBRD's regulations, were laid out in greater detail in a speech of his at the Royal Institute for International Affairs on 22 October 1991. In this speech, entitled 'Economic implications of transformation in the Soviet Union: what policy options exist?', Attali spoke first of the belief that the transformation, political and economic, of the Soviet Union was one of the 'most exciting historic processes of this century ... to see how the ideals of and practice of democracy and the market economy will take hold in a country that has little experience of either'.[39] Nonetheless, Attali continued to stress the economic problems associated with the transformation of the Soviet economy. These problems included a 13 per cent decline in gross national product (GNP) and a 9 per cent drop in industrial output, not to mention the various deficits that cumulatively totalled 320 million roubles, hyperinflation and a massive decline in imports and exports.[40]

Attali outlined a programme for the EBRD and what the rest of the industrialized First World could do to aid this great transformation project. The EBRD's initiatives were categorized into privatization and private sector development; financial sector; agricultural distribution systems; and energy. It would oversee such developments as a European School for Privatization and Management, to be located in St Petersburg, and the privatization, on a demonstration scale, of ten to twenty small and three to five large firms.[41] In the case of the latter, Attali spoke of the world-wide trend to free trade, as seen by the creation of an 'economic space' by the European Free Trade Association (EFTA) and the EC, the North American Free Trade talks and the possibility of a similar agreement in Asia. He said that this move to open trade and to tear down trade barriers should encompass all CEECs as well as the Soviet Union, through the creation of a Continental Common Market ('CORUS'), which would be like EFTA and lead to the merging of the EC and the Council for Mutual Economic Assistance (CMEA) by the year 2010.[42] With a coordinating mechanism for the Soviet Union being created with representatives from the EBRD, EC, IMF, Organization for Economic Cooperation and Development (OECD) and World Bank, and the political will in place to make CORUS work, Eastern Europe would enjoy better food prices and a higher standard of living; moreover, it would enable 'all of Europe to unite on the basis of the same economic and political ideals, without humiliating bilateral negotiations and without slowing down integration among the 12 [of the EC]'.[43]

However, Attali was continually blocked in this request to change the rules governing the status of the Soviet Union. This lack of progress was due, in part at least, to the rules governing the ability of the Bank to change its own rules. The guidelines of the EBRD are clear in that an 85 per cent majority vote is required to change the lending/borrowing requirements of any one shareholder. Consequently, the United States, along with Japan and possibly the United Kingdom, would be able to block any move to allow the Soviet Union greater leeway in its borrowing. This situation remained until the demise of the Soviet Union and its rebirth as the democratic Russian Federation.

Thus the issues pertaining to the Soviet Union are ana-chronistic because of the changes that have occurred to the Soviet Union. The Russian Federation, as a full member of the EBRD, enjoys the same rights, duties and benefits as every other member-state. However, and like the other issues mentioned above, the disagreements concerning the Soviet Union – its membership and share rights – illustrate what were perceived as 'litmus tests' for both the United States and its European counterparts in the early days of the EBRD. *The Times* posited these disagreements 'highlight a more general division among the bank's shareholders over the precise role it should play in the reconstruction of Eastern Europe'.[44]

A 'political' bank?

The Times was correct in that certain issues that plagued the EBRD at its inception indicate much about the way in which its member-states perceived its future role vis-à-vis the states of Central and Eastern Europe. Underlying the questions of whether or not the Soviet Union should be a member-state, or for that matter the EIB, and what was the appropriate number of votes for the European countries was a larger issue. This was whether or not the EBRD should be a 'bank' in the regular sense of the word, or whether it should be a 'bank' in a political sense, with a much larger, and potentially more important, role.

The EBRD *Political aspects* document mentioned above, and the link between politics and economics, pushes the EBRD in a slightly different direction from any other merchant bank and even from other international financial agencies, such as the IMF and World Bank. Attali took this 'political' aspect to heart by appearing at many forums that were not the natural domain of the EBRD. Examples of these moves by Attali are the papers he delivered on topics relating European unity, a common market for the continent, the environment and the prospect for change in Central and Eastern Europe. The last was given at the United Nations Conference on the Environment and Development. The 'politicization' of the EBRD included Attali's meeting with Gorbachev, addressing the issue of the safety of the nuclear reactors of Eastern Europe and giving press statements regarding political happenings in Central and Eastern Europe. For example, the EBRD issued a statement with respect to the appointment of a new president in Poland after much political bargaining in the first week of July 1992.[45]

But this is Attali, and what this book is more concerned with is the attitudes of the Western Europeans and how they differ from those of the United States. Thus, while Attali is important because he was the President of the Bank, there is the question of whether he represented the opinions of the member-states of the EBRD. For the latter, one must direct one's attention to the directors from Western Europe and the EC itself. The most significant Western European members of the EBRD are by far the German, French, UK and Italian governments, for they hold more influence, status and power than the other members of the EU and the EBRD in terms of voting rights in the former and rights and stock in the latter.

President Mitterrand's statement at the opening of the EBRD, even when taken with some hesitancy in one's ability to utilize it as the entirety of the French position, does at least aid in one's quest to understand that position. At the signing of the EBRD's charter Mitterrand, as noted before, remarked that 'gradually we will see, in reality, in the field, and among men and women, the development of the great Europe ... the Europe of history and geography, the Europe, you, ladies and gentlemen, represent in your vast majority. It is this Europe that we hope to build, that we want to build.'[46] Mitterrand repeated this idea of what the Bank should become when he addressed the Board of Directors on 17 July 1991. At that time, the President of France stated that 'the Bank will be active in many areas: finance, economics, even political affairs'.[47] He continued by asserting later on that he was 'delighted' to appear before the Board 'not just because you are a Bank – for there are lots of other Banks in the neighborhood – but because you have a special mission, something that only you can do, that the Bretton Woods institutions cannot do. And I am convinced that you will succeed.'[48] Not a year later, this 'vision' of the institution was repeated by Michel Sapin, the new French Governor to the Bank, during the Governor's statements at the annual general meeting. There he concluded that the 'EBRD is one of the forums in which the Europe of tomorrow is taking shape'.[49] If nothing else, this could be seen as a call to others to lend to the EBRD a 'mission' that extends far beyond that of its written mandate, as expressed in the charter of the Bank itself. Representatives of some of the other leading European countries expressed similar sentiments with respect to the importance of the EBRD. Also at the inauguration, Theo Waigel, the Finance Minister of Germany, said that EBRD has a 'very important task to perform; not only must funds be raised ... but conditions must be created under which the productive forces in the recipient countries themselves can be developed and reinforced. This is not a technocratic but a deeply political task.'[50] Similarly, the Italian Minister of the Treasury, Guido Carli, continued on this theme when he said that while, in the end, the EBRD 'remains a financial intermediator ... the Bank certainly has an important political role as a forum for East–West cooperation'.[51]

Bank staff who are on 'loan' from the State, Commerce and Treasury Departments of the US government as well as the National Security Council generally perceive that the EBRD should have a very limited scope, and that it should be restricted to what the US government perceives to be a very narrowly defined mandate as written into its charter and its first articles of functions, purposes, guidelines and objectives. This mandate is to concentrate almost entirely on private or merchant banking. One staff member did say, with respect to this belief, that 'everything the Bank does should be directed towards private enterprises ... a road should be built for a private trucking company firm to use to make money'. Thus there 'should be no larger role for the Bank beyond its mandate'.[52]

This definition of the Bank's mandate on the part of the United States is strengthened by the speeches of Nicholas Brady at the inaugural meeting of the EBRD and US officials at the institution itself. In Brady's speech during the closed session for heads of state or their representatives, he concentrated on the 'need to pursue fiscal and monetary policies which support low-inflation growth ... [and] to be vigilant against inflation ... and make a success of the Uruguay round [of GATT]'.[53] In his remarks during the open session, Brady spoke of the importance of the private sector provisions of the EBRD's charter and how this was a 'critical element of US Government support ... [and therefore] we believe strongly that the EBRD focus should be private sector development and financing of infrastructure which directly supports private sector activity'.[54] Continental Europeans were talking about 'political' concepts, the future growth and development of Europe as a whole, the breaking down of barriers between old enemies and the EBRD being the 'first institution of the new world order'. In contrast, Brady spoke of worsening US–EC relations and the need to pursue vigorous low-inflationary economic, monetary and fiscal policies. To say that the European and US delegates were not of one mind with respect to the future implications of the EBRD may be to state the obvious, but it should be noted just the same.

An independent researcher on a six-month project at the Bank gave a third-party view of this private sector 'culture' that the United States is attempting to instil at the EBRD. The researcher said that 'the US wanted to go out and create a corporate culture from the very beginning via the Merchant Banking sector of the bank with the ideas of freedom through free markets ... thus there was a business-oriented approach to lending proposals and the actual lending that has been done as to date'.[55] Added to this, the EBRD is not seen by the United States as an avenue for some of the members of the EBRD, namely some of the republics of the Commonwealth of Independent States (CIS), and Russia in particular, to gain membership of other international financial, economic and political organizations such as the IMF and the World Bank. This is in direct contrast to views held by the French and German governments, and President Attali, as seen by his invitation to Gorbachev and his asking the G-7 leaders to invite Gorbachev to a G-7 summit. The researcher's proof of his assertions comes not only from being able to research the internal memorandums, closed meetings and directors of the EBRD, but from US actions at the EBRD and other similar international financial institutions. He said that the move to stop some of the policy ideas of Attali and some of the member-states of the EC was for both pragmatic and ideological reasons. This will be highlighted in starker terms later in this chapter with respect to Brady's response to Attali's ideas concerning the establishment of 'soft loans'.

Same story, different venue

The same approach was and continues to be true of the US government's attitude towards other multilateral developmental banks, such as the Inter-American Development Bank and the World Bank.[56] The latter is a prime example of US policy for two reasons. The first is that the scope of the World Bank is international and the second reason is that the most recent debate over the World Bank's mandate and functions blossomed in March 1991. What makes this time frame interesting is that the EBRD was almost ready to begin business at the same time, thus the negotiations for that developmental bank were occurring at the same time as the debate about the World Bank.

In the case of the World Bank, the incoming president, Lewis Preston, was faced with a challenge, led mainly by the United States, that had as its desired outcome a change in the manner in which the Bank conducts its business. *The Economist*, in a March 1991 column, gave a brief overview of the ensuing debate. The journal stated that it was centred around the ability, or lack thereof, of the institution to lend to the private sector and whether or not the Bank would do a better job if its articles of purpose were changed not merely to allow it to loan to the private sector, but to bias loans towards this sector of the economy in preference to the public sector.[57]

This debate arose when the International Finance Corporation (IFC), the private sector division of the World Bank group, but not a direct part of the Bank itself, wanted to double its capital with an extra $1.3 billion from its shareholders. However, the US Treasury objected to this, saying that the IFC should talk to governments about policy. The *Financial Times* commented that if the IFC did so, then the World Bank would be 'obligated' to talk to governments less, freeing it up to talk to private enterprises more. A member of staff within the US administration was,

within the same context, able to highlight the United States'
objection to the World Bank generally when he said that 'we like
the IFC. We think it does a good job, but we think [that] it should
[be] more private sector oriented and has not done enough in
emphasizing privatization'.[58] The debate surrounding the reform-
ation of the IFC and World Bank delayed the approval of a further
$1.3 billion being allocated to a number of Third World projects.
Nonetheless, another US official stated that for the United States
it was 'more important to get the reforms than for the IFC to lose
a few transactions'.[59]

By June 1991 it appeared that an agreement between the Bank,
the IFC and the United States had been reached for the doubling
of the capital pool of the IFC. David Mulford, a US Treasury
under-secretary, commented in a press statement that this new
capital must be 'part of an accelerated effort by the entire World
Bank group to support private sector development'.[60] A follow-
on from this agreement was a new programme introduced at the
Bank intended to broaden the scope of the Enhanced Co-
financing Operation (ECO). This enlargement of the mandate of
the ECO, as posited by Frank Gray, was to make it easier for
commercial banks to participate in the financing of aid projects in
developing countries.[61] In essence it was a measure that had as its
intent the buttressing of aid programmes and which sought to
'broaden the potential for private sector equity participation in
infrastructure projects'.[62]

Another third party corroborated this postulation that there
are ideological differences between the United States and the
continental European governments. One high-level official at the
EBRD, from one of the Central European states most likely to
achieve a successful transformation of its political and economic
systems, also reflected upon the role of the United States in
various international institutions like the World Bank and the
IMF, and the related direction of these organizations. There was a

none-too-veiled link between the economic ideology of the IMF in particular, which is one of pure market economics, and the fact that the United States is its most influential member. The official then noted that, in his opinion, there was a strong bias in most of Europe towards a social orientation that permits the interaction of the state and the economy while 'in the United States this is less possible'.[63] While not said in so many words, the official clearly pointed to a perception that is widely held by many of his colleagues from the rest of Central and Eastern Europe. This perception is that there is a distinct difference between the Americans and Western Europeans with respect to the role that the state should play in the economic affairs of a country. Though not judging which was better than the other, the official did say that while there was a turn to 'market economies without adjectives', as Vaclav Klaus, the former Czech Prime Minister, called them, all of these countries would eventually move back from an extreme free market position to a point somewhere in the middle and establish some equilibrium between the role of the market and that of the state. This would be the case because all of these countries, especially those in Central Europe, are at heart socially oriented and thus will come to resemble a German-styled economic system more than a US one. The traditions of these countries are European rather than American and thus they will develop accordingly.[64]

However, and with respect to the EBRD, US government staff do assert that this institution, almost aside from the above, is a *political* institution first and foremost. They contend that the US government does view the EBRD as such and that therefore branches of the executive are in the lead with respect to relationships with the EBRD. Most of the staff on loan from the United States come from the State Department, the National Security Council, Commerce Department and Treasury, in that order. As such, the EBRD for these people and the US government itself is 'political' rather than 'economic'. However, this leads to two questions that must be tackled. The first is why, if the State Department is in the 'lead', should the Secretary for the Treasury speak as the representative for the United States at EBRD assemblies such as the first annual general meeting, instead of the Secretary of State? If indeed the United States agrees to the link between politics and economics, as seen by the mandate of the EBRD and the section of the executive that is supposedly in the 'lead', then the second question is whether the US government holds the same view of what 'political' means as continental Western Europeans?

People within the President's office maintain, as has been espoused above, that the US government does place more emphasis on the private than on the public/developmental sector of the EBRD and joint ventures and those sorts of projects.[65] These same staff also noted that, in their opinion, it appears that the United States does not believe that being 'political' is about issuing press statements and talking about issues that do not fall within the limited mandate of the institution, such as nuclear reactor safety and continental and world-wide trade developments. 'Political' for the US government appears to be understood simply in terms of sanctioning countries when they fail to meet the 'democracy' tests of the guidelines and rules of the EBRD. One staff member stated that if the Bank, and Attali in particular, stayed within these latter and more limiting definitions of 'political', then a consensus could be reached between the US and its Western European allies on the political nature of the EBRD.[66]

Solutions?

Compromises between Western Europe and the United States were necessary for the EBRD to become operational. Thus, divergences were smoothed over in all areas, and most importantly with respect to those concerns related to the economic philosophy of the institution. To summarize from the above, it was agreed that the EIB should be allowed to become an independent shareholder, but with only 3 per cent of the total one million shares. However, while it was agreed that the EIB could hold independent shares in the EBRD, the chairman's report in the *Basic documents of the EBRD* states that this status should not be interpreted as a 'precedent for other organisations or Banks to become members of the Bank [EBRD], or that their membership would be used as a precedent for them to become members of other organisations or other banks'.[67]

Other compromises, as indicated above, were reached with respect to the status of the Soviet Union, the voting shares to held by the member-states of the EC, the 'political' nature of the institution itself and the amount of capital that should be directed to 'public' and 'private' venture programmes. But were these agreements concerning the policies of the EBRD compromises, or attempts by the dominant member-states to 'fudge' on issues that they knew were unsolvable? An indication with respect to the answer lies in whether or not similar and/or related issues reappeared over time after the establishment of the EBRD.

One year on – unresolved issues

The lending policies of the EBRD received much criticism in the run-up to its first annual general meeting. Not only were some of the projects called into question because of potential conflicts of interest involving the EBRD President, Jacques Attali, but also because the EBRD had spent so little of its capital. While the Bank issued a list of projects agreed to and under negotiation,[68] the criticism remained.[69] In response, EBRD officials are quoted as saying that it had been difficult, because of the private sector lending restrictions, to find appropriate areas of investment in

CEECs, as they lacked small and medium-size enterprises and an entrepreneurial spirit among the middle classes.[70]

In response to these criticisms, Attali, at the second annual general meeting, called for the creation of a special restructuring facility that would involve itself in 'soft' loans and high-risk equity for the restructuring of heavy industry, such as the defence sector. He said that there was a 'clear need for technical assistance and training on a vast scale, and for the provision of substantial "high risk" equity investment'.[71] Because of the almost total collapse of eastern trade via the old CMEA routes and the establishment of barriers to certain Central and Eastern European goods on the part of the EC, the private sector in most CEECs was not growing as fast as most analysts had expected, and investment was compromised by the condition of many of the facilities.

The state of the Russian defence industry is only one example of this situation. Firms in this sector of the economy were 'totally unfitted to competitive conditions … [and therefore] need to be reduced to a size compatible with region requirements'.[72] This position was publicly supported by the head of the development banking division of the EBRD, the alternate governor for Italy and, most importantly, the German Minister of Finance and governor for Germany, Theo Waigel. The latter stated, in his address to the general meeting, that 'it is the EBRD's role to help organise and support a withdrawal of the all-powerful state from the economy … [but] the state must be put in a position enabling it to carry out its tasks efficiently'.[73] Consequently, in order for the EBRD to accomplish these objectives, a special restructuring programme was required. Attali stated in his address to the meeting that:

> privatisation and enterprise creation are far too slow; at the present rate it would take two generations to achieve a private sector share comparable to that of Western Europe … the

absence of healthy banking and financial institutions ... lack of access to international capital markets ... absence of convertible currency ... are many of the reasons for this ... in fact, entire sectors need to be restructured before any thought can be given to privatising them ... [and] a case in point is the defence industry ... for this purpose we should like, with you, to set up a *Special Restructuring Programme*, which will finance such projects from a new kind of resources.[74]

For many associated with the EBRD, this call for a special restructuring facility, involving high-risk equity investments and so-called soft loans because of their low interest rates and lenient credit terms, signalled a shift away from the private/ public orientation of the Bank to one that would be more 'developmental'. This perception was not lost on the US Secretary of the Treasury, Nicholas Brady. In response to the Attali speech and restructuring proposal, he said in his address that the EBRD:

cannot cover the entire range of needs; it cannot be all things to all people; it cannot hope to cover all factors, both private and public, in all countries. In this regard we [the US] are not convinced of the need to branch into new restructuring oper- ations involving major policy changes that detract from the bank's main mission ... don't recapitalise state owned enter- prises. Recapitalising money-losing operations won't get the job done.[75]

With respect to the purely 'ideological' component to Brady's rejection of the special restructuring programme, he stressed at the annual general meeting that any move into 'pure' develop- mental banking would be a 'diversion of the EBRD's efforts'. He then mentioned that this move to a greater focus on develop- mental banking through the 'soft loan' approach would 'dilute the "special" focus of the bank which is more [in the eyes of the US administration] of a merchant market-driven approach'.[76]

Theo Waigel, who at the same meeting was elected president of the Board of Governors,[77] stated that a consensus among Board members had been reached, in that privatization should be encouraged, but only when conditions became acceptable. Consequently, President Attali's restructuring plans would be studied in detail to see if they would be useful in meeting the objectives of the EBRD and the requirements of CEECs.[78] Again, and like the negotiations prior to the establishment of the EBRD, a compromise had been reached to 'fudge' issues that the dominant member-states had concluded to be unsolvable, because they concerned strongly held beliefs with respect to models of economic development and the role of the state in this development.

Disagreements, disagreements, disagreements

One EBRD official commented that issues relating to the economic philosophy of the Bank, such as the 'soft loan' policy, were inevitably going to be the 'dividing line between the Continental Europeans and the Anglo-Saxon countries, as well as the Japanese'.[79] This assertion reflects external opinion that what was occurring between the majority of the member-states of the EC and the United States was a clash of ideologies that underlay three 'fundamental differences in philosophy about the nature of economic reform in Eastern Europe'.[80] The first concerned the method of economic reform; the second whether privatization should occur before or after the restructuring of certain industries; and the third whether these processes required additional funds.

For the Reagan and Bush administrations, free market capitalism dictated that privatization was the key to unlocking the economies of Central and Eastern Europe, whereas the

majority of Western Europe was not as adamant that the free
market was the only option available to these countries. Nonetheless, one German official working at the EBRD stated that
Germany and other continental Western European countries
were never 'in favor of having written down a strict division of
how financial resources should be invested'.[81] Instead, it was the
US government that was persistent in its desire to codify its free
market beliefs within the confines of the EBRD. One possible
reason for this interest in codification was the US attitude, as
stated previously, that 'European policy-makers … are indifferent,
if not hostile, to growth economies … [and] still think that
socialism can be reformed'.[82]

Many of the people associated with the EBRD who have been
interviewed conclude that there are differences between the
continental member-states of the EC and the United States
and United Kingdom, particularly with respect to economic
philosophies and, thus, the direction of the EBRD. One example
of the Europeans' less doctrinaire approach is illustrated by the
comments of one Western European official on secondment to the
EBRD. This official noted that there was the perception, inside the
EBRD, that for the Europeans 'the state has a natural role in
economic governance … [and] state-owned enterprises are a
natural way of organising economic activity'.[83] The overt involvement of most Western European states in the management and
ownership of aspects of their respective economies, compared
with the lack of overt involvement by government in the United
States, is an indication of the 'correctness' of this perception.
Similarly, US officials on secondment to the EBRD noted that the
leadership and political elite of the United States have a 'different
view than those of the Europeans with regard to the role of the
public sector of and in the economy'.[84] To this end, there is an
'ideological bent' towards the prioritization of privatization and
the private sectors of economies that is 'characteristic of the

political discourse within the United States'.[85] Notably, this comment was made with reference to the debate between President Attali and Secretary Brady concerning Attali's proposal for a special restructuring programme.

Conclusions

What can one take from the above exploration of the initial year of operations at the EBRD? It is safe to conclude that while there was a degree of cooperation and agreement with respect to some of the principles of the EBRD, it was an institution replete with a sense of 'fudging' with respect to the most fundamental and important issues pertaining to its operations and day-to-day administration. The personal interviews, coupled with speeches from the representatives of the leading countries of the EBRD and its major protagonists, as well as what actually was agreed to, illustrate an institution fraught with not only pragmatic and political disputes but also highly ideological and 'idea-based' ones as well. The status of the EIB and the Soviet Union, the debates over public/private lending orientation and the mirroring of these debates in the World Bank/IFC, and the debacle over restructuring or privatization and the 'soft loans' initiative of Attali all highlight this divide that the newspapers, commentators, EBRD staff and directors have alluded to, spoken of and recognized as the fundamental concern at the EBRD.

But how can the presence and import of these 'ideas' be explained? Can traditional theories of international relations adequately assist in the development of an explanation for these 'ideas-based' disagreements? Can one better understand the building of institutions through these traditional theories, or will there be a need to turn to paradigms that are more 'critical' in their approach? Having laid the groundwork – having illustrated the presence of disagreement at the level of ideas as well at the level of the practical, pragmatic and political – the task of the next chapter is to work towards the development of an *explanation* of these disagreements, if in fact an explanation can be found.

Notes

1 EC, *Bulletin of the European Community*, EC 12–1989, pp. 14–15.

2 See Appendices C and D for the initial (1990) and present-day (1999) membership list of the EBRD.

3 EBRD, personal interviews, 1992.

4 EBRD, *Basic documents of the European Bank for Reconstruction and Development*, 29 May 1990, article 1.

5 See Appendix E for the first articles of the EBRD.

6 'A new bank plans East European aid', *NYT*, 30 May 1990, p. A14.

7 'Mitterrand says EBRD is step to united Europe', *Financial Times (FT)*, 16 April 1990, p. 1.

8 EBRD, statement by Jacques Attali, *Blueprint*, 18 December 1991.

9 *Ibid.*, p. 20.

10 EBRD, *Annual general report*, March 1992, pp. 9–10.

11 EBRD, *Political aspects of the mandate of the European Bank for Reconstruction and Development*, 1991, p. 2.

12 EBRD, *Basic documents*.

13 *Ibid.*, article 11.

14 See Appendix F for selected text of *Political aspects of the EBRD*.

15 S. Weber, 'Origins of the European Bank for Reconstruction and Development', *International Organization*, Vol. 48, No. 1, 1994, p. 32.

16 EC, *Bulletin of the European Community*, EC–12 1989, pp. 12–13.

17 P. Menkveld, *Origin and role of the European Bank for Reconstruction and Development*, London: Graham and Trotman, 1992, p. 61.

18 US Foreign Bureau of Information Services, 'US role in Reconstruction Bank viewed', 28 June 1990, pp. 1–2.

19 P. Menkveld, *Origin and role*, p. 61.

20 *Ibid.*, p. 62.

21 'Industrial nations to create bank to aid Eastern Europe', *NYT*, 10 April 1990, p. D2.

22 EBRD, personal interviews, 1993.

23 Menkveld, *Origin and role*, p. 62.

24 EBRD, personal interviews, 1993.

25 EBRD, personal interviews, 1992.

26 EBRD, personal interviews, 1993.

27 EBRD, *Basic documents*, article 11.
28 *Ibid*.
29 EC, *Official Journal of the European Community*, 25 October 1989, p. 149.
30 'Bush rejects lending to the Soviet Union', *FT*, 19 March 1990, p. 2.
31 EBRD, personal interviews, 1992.
32 Menkveld, *Origin and role*, p. 56.
33 'US hard line on aid for Russia', *The Times*, 16 March 1990, p. 8.
34 Menkveld, *Origin and role*, p. 60.
35 *Ibid*.
36 'Attali calls for the easing of EBRD restrictions on Soviet Union', *FT*, 17 June 1991, p. 1.
37 EBRD, personal interviews, 1992.
38 'Attali calls for the easing of EBRD restrictions on Soviet Union', *FT*.
39 J. Attali, 'Economic implications of transformation in the Soviet Union: what policy options exist?', EBRD, 22 October 1991, p. 3.
40 *Ibid*., pp. 5–6.
41 *Ibid*., p. 12.
42 *Ibid*., p. 14.
43 *Ibid*., p. 15.
44 'Attali shelves his soft loans', *The Times*, 14 April 1992, p. 21.
45 EBRD, Information Office, 1992.
46 'Mitterrand says EBRD is step to united Europe', *FT*, 16 April 1990, p. 1.
47 EBRD, *Blueprint*, 18 December 1991, p. 30.
48 *Ibid*.
49 EBRD, *Blueprint*, 12 May 1992, p. 4.
50 *Ibid*., p. 28.
51 *Ibid*., p. 33.
52 EBRD, personal interviews, 1992.
53 EBRD, *Proceedings of the first annual general meeting of the EBRD*, April 1991, p. 30.
54 *Ibid*., p. 121.
55 EBRD, personal interviews, 1992.
56 See Weber, 'Origins of the European Bank for Reconstruction and Development', pp. 28–33.
57 'A job for Atlas and Hercules', *The Economist*, 30 March 1991, p. 93.
58 'US urges World Bank policy shift', *FT*, 19 April 1991, p. 24.
59 'US press for change in focus at World Bank', *The Times*, 22 April 1991, p. 20.
60 'US supports rise in capital for IFC', *FT*, 13 June 1991, p. 6.
61 F. Gray, 'World Bank approves new co-financing tool', *FT*, 22 November 1991, p. 7.
62 *Ibid*.
63 EBRD, personal interviews, 1992.

64 *Ibid.*

65 *Ibid.*

66 *Ibid.*

67 EBRD, *Chairman's report on the agreement establishing the EBRD*, 29 May 1990, article 3. See EBRD, *Basic documents*, for text.

68 EBRD, *Blueprint*, 18 December 1992 and 12 May 1992.

69 *The Economist*, 'Growing pains at the Eurobank', 28 March 1992, pp. 107–8.

70 *Ibid.* See also EBRD Board of Governors, 'Small and medium enterprises', April 1993, unpublished paper.

71 See J. Attali, in EBRD, *Proceedings of the second annual general meeting*, 13–15 April 1992.

72 *Ibid.*

73 EBRD, *Proceedings of the second annual general meeting*, 13–15 April 1992, p. 62.

74 EBRD, statement by J. Attali in *Blueprint*, 12 May 1992, p. 5. The EBRD published an unofficial two-volume report on defence industries in CEECs and the Soviet Union, claiming that what was required first was a restructuring of plants so that privatization could then occur.

75 Quoted in *The Times*, 'Brady attacks ambitions of EBRD', 14 April 1992, p. 1.

76 EBRD, statement by Attali in *Blueprint*, 12 May 1992, p. 5.

77 The EBRD has both a Board of Governors and a Board of Directors. The former consists of the highest-level political representation for each member-state of the EBRD. In theory, this is the prime minister or president, but in reality countries are represented at this level by the treasury or state departments. For example, the United States has been represented by Robert Rubin, Secretary of State for the Treasury, or one of his under-secretaries. The Board of Directors is the most senior day-to-day level of management at the EBRD. Each member-state is represented and has a voting power equivalent to its number of shares. Decisions undertaken include all potential project activity of the institution as well as some policy matters, such as organizational structure. This may include the hiring of some senior staff, but not the President. That, as well as the finalization of major policy issues such as lending criteria, is the domain of the Board of Governors.

78 EBRD, *Proceedings of the second annual general meeting*, 13–15 April 1992, p. 62.

79 EBRD, personal interviews, 1993.

80 *The Times*, 'Attali shelves his soft loans', 14 April 1992, p. 21.

81 EBRD, personal interviews, 1992.

82 *Ibid.*

83 EBRD, personal interviews, 1992.

84 *Ibid.*

85 *Ibid.*

4

1991 and onwards – a new beginning or old news?

Introduction

The EBRD was marked by a contrast of almost complete disagreement and sometimes total agreement among the dominant Western states. This chapter seeks to explore the possible reasons for this within the context of the EBRD since the end of 1992 on both practical and theoretical levels of reasoning. The goal is to locate these changes within the context of a theoretical paradigm that may be able to assist one's understanding of harmonious change inside institutions under pressure to change. To this end, the chapter will briefly recount the criticisms directed at this institution from its inception up to the end of 1992. It will also posit theoretical explanations for this turn of events and combine these positions with personal accounts of the operations of the EBRD from officials at the institution. A return to the theoretical will then ask whether any of these initial criticisms can be sustained and if not, why not. An alternative theoretical position will be advanced in the next chapter, as will a brief assessment of how these institutional changes have assisted, or hindered, the process of transition in Central and Eastern Europe.

The criticism

The previous chapter has indicated that the EBRD was being
roundly condemned for not loaning enough capital to ventures in
Central and Eastern Europe. A number of prominent politicians
from the region downplayed the role of the EBRD, with one
asserting that the role of the Bank, at the end of 1992, had been
marginal, at best.[1] With but 200 million ECU lent by the end of
that year, even senior officials from the EBRD were quoted as
saying that 'the bank is going to take a more proactive approach
in the future'.[2] In truth, the EBRD had seen a remarkable increase
in the amount of capital it had loaned to companies, as opposed
to public sector projects, by the end of 1992 compared with the
previous year. EBRD records illustrate that in 1991, 200 million
ECU were loaned, while 740 million ECU were assigned the next
year to forty-two different investments.[3]

The EBRD was also criticized for spending too much on itself
and, when it did loan money, for lending to the wrong types of
ventures. First, the organization moved to a new location in the
City of London and spent vast sums on this refit, which included
marble floors. Simultaneously, it was discovered that even though
the EBRD had actually spent very little on projects in the
transitional states of Central and Eastern Europe, a some of these
appeared controversial. With respect to the latter, the EBRD
invested in a project that was being funded by Nestle and BSN,
two multinational companies. *The Economist* asked whether or
not the bank should 'invest in high-profile ventures with wealthy
westerners', the implication being that these companies did not
need such assistance and the capital could be better spent on
projects where the partners were small and medium-sized
businesses requiring start-up funding.[4] The same journal ques-
tioned the integrity of another venture, this one involving the
twin brother of the President of the EBRD.[5] It was, in part,

because of its thrift and apparent wrong decision making that the US representative, Nicholas Brady, stated at one of the annual general meetings that the EBRD should not try to be 'all things to all people'.[6]

A number of reasons may be cited for the lack of spending on the part of the institution in its initial years of operation. These include a combined lack of potential partners and actual capital to spend as well as having to abide by the stringent conditions agreed to by the member-states. However, given the types of deals that were concluded, as illustrated above, and the admission by senior EBRD officials that more projects could have been agreed to during those first years,[7] the future of the EBRD as it was originally constituted did not appear healthy, and nor did the position of Attali as President. By March 1994, Jacques Attali had been replaced by Jacques De Larosiere, and the institution had overhauled its administrative and decision-making processes. The number of approved projects and amount of capital spent in Central and Eastern Europe has increased year on year. In 1993, the number of projects approved rose to seventy-three and the total amount of capital to 1.7 billion ECU, and 1994 saw an increase to ninety-two projects and a similar amount of funds being allocated. As of 31 July 1995, thirty-eight new ventures had been agreed, with a total of 500 million ECU being spent by the institution.[8] In the wake of this activism and improved balanced sheet, the criticism that had plagued those first few years appears to have disappeared. Even officials on secondment to the EBRD from the United States agree that the institution is beginning to operate in a manner befitting its mandate.

The question at this juncture is why has this criticism ceased? Is it simply because the EBRD is loaning more money to more ventures than ever before, or because Jacques Attali has been forced from his position, or because the strict division between public and private has been diminished in the interest of the 'country-by-country' approach proposed by De Larosiere? Or are these changes indicative of a more fundamental shift of beliefs and concerns on the part of the leading member-states of the institution that have then been manifested in changes at the operational level? Before attempting to answer these questions, this chapter will examine the traditional manners in which cooperation between states has been understood within the context of theories of international relations.

New beginnings, theoretically speaking

Epistemic communities

In an article in *International Organization*, Peter Haas speaks of the role that 'epistemic communities' play in the bridging of gaps that occur between systemic conditions, knowledge and national actions within the context of organizations. Haas asserts that human agency, by way of knowledge-based experts, is able to influence and shape the decisions taken by national leaders or their representatives at organizations such as the EBRD.[9] As well as describing how and why organizations of all types and kinds are able to operate in the face of disagreements at the political level, Haas comments that these 'epistemic communities' allow insights into the state of the theoretical debate within international relations. Such reliance on human agency would be difficult, Haas notes, if one operated theoretically from either a neorealist or neoliberal perspective. Haas remarks that the weakness of neorealist theory is that it assumes that 'international actors or units lack even a minimal capacity for deducing different expectations from the same structural change or for reflecting on alternative models of behavior', while neoliberals exclude or ignore the 'dynamic interaction between domestic and international political games'. As a response, theorizing by way of 'epistemic communities' may allow one to 'describe these [political] games not only in terms of material interests but also as part of the bargaining and negotiating that take place among different epistemic understandings and practices'.[10]

To do justice to this theorization, let us begin by outlining Haas' definition of these epistemic communities. The author states that these are networks 'of professionals with recognized expertise and competence in a particular domain and an authoritative claim to policy-relevant knowledge within that domain or issue-area'.[11] These experts have:

1 a shared set of normative principles and beliefs, which provide a value-based rationale for the social action of community members;
2 shared causal beliefs, which are derived from their analysis of practices leading or contributing to a central set of problems in their domain and which then serve as the basis for elucidating multiple linkages between possible policy actions and desirable outcomes;
3 shared notions of validity;
4 a common policy enterprise – a set of common practices associated with a set of problems to which their professional competence is directed.[12]

Haas makes the point that any agglomeration of bureaucrats or professionals is not necessarily an epistemic community.[13] However, for the purposes of this project, and given the enterprise in which the staff at the EBRD are engaged, many of the characteristics noted above as those that define an epistemic community are shared at the Bank. One might therefore conclude that its staff comprise such a community. Coupled with this anecdotal evidence is Haas' admission that bureaucratic bodies and epistemic communities, while different, do 'share a focus on administrative empowerment of specialized knowledge groups'.[14]

What appears to be crucial to the utilization of this approach to international organizations is not so much that such communities exist, but what they may be able to do, given their ability to control the flow of information in a multitude of directions. Haas comments that it is true that this ability to determine policies and affect outcomes is limited by the structures in which these communities operate.[15] However, there are a number of novel ways in which these communities *can* affect policy. Chiefly, epistemic communities may be able to assist in the creation of new patterns of behaviour and 'prove to be an important determinant of international policy coordination'.[16] Also, and at the level of the state, the leadership of a given state may elect to pursue new objectives in part because of the distribution of power capabilities but also because of the distribution of information.[17]

Finally, Haas indicates the ways in which these communities are able to influence and determine policy actions and outcomes. In the areas of policy innovation, diffusion, selection, persistence and 'policy learning as evolution', epistemic communities are able to determine, to a greater or lesser extent, the range of policies that enter and exit the decision-making process of an institution.[18] Without going into detail, Haas believes that at almost every point along the decision-making process, save for the final point at which a decision is made, epistemic communities have a tremendous amount of influence over how that decision will be made. In turn, these communities are able consciously to limit the range of policies that could be accepted and then implemented by senior management.

It is this ability, or possible ability, of epistemic communities to control the decision-making process that influences the work of Peter Haas and like-minded academics.[19] However, this interest must be taken within a certain setting, which is for Haas the paucity of literature within international relations that is able adequately to explain the sources of international institutions, state interests and state behaviour under conditions of uncertainty.[20] Haas, as mentioned above, critiques neorealist, game theoretic, neofunctional, cognitive and neoliberal perspectives in their attempt to explain this triangular relationship. Neorealism lacks the ability to differentiate between actors and detach itself from its systemic-level analysis, whereas game theoretic approaches abstract out the individual and international levels of analysis, two of the key levels of analysis in Haas' approach.[21] Neoliberal approaches end where Haas and his colleagues begin. The latter are attempting to go beyond a material capabilities-based approach to international institutions and be inclusive of the bargaining and negotiating that occurs between and within epistemic communities. An appreciation of the role that 'collective understandings' play in the formulation of policy approaches by these communities is also another point that separates Haas and neoliberal theorists.[22] Finally, neofunctional and cognitive approaches, such as those advanced by Ernst Haas and John Gerard Ruggie, are very useful, but also are to be found lacking. Instead of asking how loyalties are shifting from one authority to another because of some scientific reasoning, this research into epistemic communities asks *'Who learns what, when, to whose benefit, and why?'*.[23] This, therefore, is a learning-based approach, rather than one which is science-based.

The above criticism of the approach taken by traditional theories of international relations with respect to the triangular relationship between states, state behaviour and international institutions is damning, as well as broadly based. However, we would be amiss if a similar amount of space was not accorded to the more 'accepted' of these traditional theories. To this end, the neorealist/game theoretic and neoliberal/new institutional approaches to this relationship will be examined prior to a detailed examination of the dramatic changes that have occurred within the EBRD since the end of 1992.

Anarchy and *cooperation*

Few neorealists would not adhere to the twin propositions that states, in comparison with non-state actors such as international organizations, are the primary actors in international relations, and that with respect to the long-standing 'agency–structure' debate, the former is more important in the calculations of the national interests of a primary actor than the latter.[24] To this end, the criticisms of this perspective by Peter Haas point towards why he concludes that neorealist theorists are unable properly to explain the triangular relationship between states, state behaviour and international institutions. While these theorists are able to account for the first two aspects of this relationship, the proposition that states are the primary actors internationally, and that international organizations are therefore not autonomous actors, disables these theorists from completing the triangle.

However, within this framework a number of important pieces of work have been written with respect to why and how states do cooperate with each other, and at times do so within the confines of international organizations. Kenneth Oye, in an article entitled 'Explaining cooperation under anarchy', posits that cooperation is understandable especially if two actors are located within an iterated context. After reviewing the three common 'game' structures – chicken, prisoner's dilemma and stag hunt – the author concluded that on a non-iterated basis there would be a lack of circumstances that would suggest cooperation between two like-minded power-seeking actors in a state of uncertainty and anarchy.[25] The circumstance that would alter state preferences would therefore be a scenario that would operate on an iterated basis. Because these actors would have to meet again, there would be a stronger interest to cooperate, at least on a minimal level, rather than to disagree. What has changed is the future, or specifically that there will be a future relationship between these actors. Accordingly, both are concerned with each other's reliability, a character trait that provokes like responses.[26] This so-called 'shadow of the future' alters the preferences of the actors in question, thus reconfiguring the outcome of the relationship itself.[27]

These preferences are what Robert Jervis speaks of in his article 'Realism, game theory and cooperation'. Preferences, for Jervis, come in many forms, including transnational forces, systemic structures, the ideologies and beliefs of the individual decision makers and those which are taken as givens by game theoretic models. The process of interaction between actors, one's changing experience and knowledge can also alter these preferences.[28] Problematic for Haas is that Jervis openly criticizes those tendencies in realism/game theory that take as given or define as exogenous to an understanding of cooperation between actors experience, knowledge and the range of preferences listed above.[29] Jervis cites beliefs, values and other psychological perceptions as possible impediments to cooperation between actors. Realism and game theory tend to ignore or devalue these factors in the search for a parsimonious theoretical position.[30] Jervis, however, is of the opinion that these factors are real and therefore need to be examined further. The author states that 'what is crucial in determining whether the actors cooperate is their beliefs about the effectiveness of alternative policies'.[31]

Nonetheless, the position of realism/game theory is that these concerns are not examined, are taken as givens and are assumed both to have been factored into one's calculation of rational interests and to be representative not of personal beliefs but those of a 'national self'.[32] Consequently, the choices made by decision makers are those made from a utilitarian perspective concerned with the self-interested needs of the primary actor (the state) that they represent. While knowledge and other like factors, such as the role of 'epistemic communities', may be important in the calculation of these interests, these are still interests that remain influenced by objective and rational factors such as the place that a given state occupies in the international system and its material/physical capabilities and resources. Therefore cooperation occurs when the international environment a state is located within is such that cooperation, or a change from conflict to cooperation, is the rational and logical decision to be made, irrespective of institutions or the presence of epistemic communities.

This lack of interest in either has recently been espoused by John Mearsheimer in a series of articles in *International Security*. Mearsheimer contends that, at their core, realist theorists believe that 'institutions cannot get states to stop behaving as short-term power-maximizers … [and therefore] reflect state calculations of self-interest based primarily on concerns of relative power'.[33] He adds that while institutions may be useful in the maintenance or increase of the power of a given state or group of states, they do not have 'significant independent effects on state behavior'.[34] In response to correspondence by Robert Keohane, John Gerard Ruggie and Alexander Wendt, Mearsheimer contends that none of them answers the central question of his initial argument, which is:

> can international institutions prevent war by changing state behavior … can institutions push states away from war by getting them to eschew balance-of-power logic, and to refrain from calculating each important move according to how it affects their relative power position?[35]

With respect to the theoretical position most relevant to this discussion, Mearsheimer criticizes Robert Keohane and others for being 'realists by any other name' while still claiming to be institutionalists, when the latter states that the difference between institutionalism and realism is not the independent or dependent status of institutions, but concerns why they were created and how they affect states. Mearsheimer also contends that Keohane is using the language of realism, for if institutions are not independent actors then their ability to affect state behaviour is limited.[36] Finally, Mearsheimer criticizes the use of political economic examples, asserting that oil pollution regimes tell one very little about war and peace issues.[37] Given that the subject of this book is the EBRD, a *political economic* organization, it might appear that, on the surface, realist thought may have little to add to one's understanding of the present realities of the EBRD. This position, after an analysis of the EBRD, may or may not be true. Judgement on this matter will be reserved until a later chapter.

Institutionalism and change

The neoliberal or complex interdependent position of Robert Keohane may be said to begin where realism and game theory end. This position does not take for granted nor does it assume a priority place for states in international politics. A realistic view of world politics indicates that while states are the dominant actors, they are far from being the only important ones. International institutions of all kinds, as well as other non-state, non-institutional actors, are not only present but at times operate as autonomous creatures. To deny this fact would be the denial of reality, or at least reality as Keohane perceives it to be.[38]

But this acceptance of reality does not inform one with respect to the questions of how and, more importantly why, these institutional arrangements, formal and informal, are agreed to.[39]

Simply put, neoliberals ask the same question as game theorists, which is why do states cooperate. The answer is that there are a number of 'costs' to international relations that are deemed to be too expensive for states to bear independently of each other. The cost of certain transactions, the desire to attain as much information as possible that is 'perfect' and a demand for a clear framework of guidelines are the factors cited by Keohane as the primary reasons why international regimes and institutions are created.[40] The attainment of a greater degree of certainty in an anarchic world is the payoff for the states that decide to cooperate with each other. States still act in a rational and logical manner with respect to the national self-interest, just as realists claim. The difference between these two positions is in the autonomy accorded these institutions and their ability, through their principles and norms, to change the calculation of state self-interest over time. Neoliberalism also differs from the 'epistemic community' position because what is not central to this position is the role played by a group of knowledge-based experts, but rather the institutional setting in which these experts are located. This is so because these institutional settings are able to change the incentives for cooperation and increase the opportunities for such incentives to appear because of the decrease in the uncertainty states face prior to making decisions. It is primarily because of this changed environment that epistemic communities are able to influence the decision-making process of a given institution.

Finally, Keohane has updated his analysis with a reply to a realist account of institutions, all to be found in *International Security*.[41] In his response to the Mearsheimer position that institutions are unable, within the context of issues relating to war and peace, to change state behaviour, Keohane replies with a multitude of suggestions. First, he stakes out the differences between institutionalism and realism, which include the proposition that when self-interested benefits for cooperation do not occur, institutions will not be created. However, when these benefits do occur, so too will institutions, regimes and alliances of *all* types.[42] By reducing transaction costs, providing information, enhancing transparency and provoking a greater degree of contact between states, these institutions can enhance the initial level of cooperation between the states in question.[43]

Second, Keohane asserts that there is no clear 'dividing line' between political economic and security (war and peace) issues, as purported by Mearsheimer. The literature in question has consistently made the claim that institutional theory can be applied to both security and political economic issues equally. This is so because one of the crucial aspects of institutions is their ability to provide information, and more 'perfect' or transparent information than that states might be able to obtain outside the institutional environment. Given that war represents the most anarchic of all situations, the benefits accrued to a state through the attainment of better information is obvious to Keohane. Consequently, it is through the receipt of this information, obtained via an independent institution, that the preferences and interests of a state can and most likely will be changed, as well as what each views as 'relative gains' between various actors.[44] In his summary, Keohane posits that it is Mearsheimer's world of war and peace that requires institutionalization, given the potential for destruction if and when states fail to cooperate at even a minimal level of coexistence. While not pretending that institutions are a panacea, they may be 'components of any lasting peace'.[45]

Stephen Krasner takes up this argument by stressing an even more autonomous and therefore important role for regimes and institutions than that of Keohane. This autonomy is derived from certain lags that occur between the preferences of member-states and the actions of the regime in question. Rather than a world characterized by billiard balls, Krasner views international relations as a series of tectonic plates moving across each other. These plates, one representing state power and the other the regime, its characteristics and outcomes, produce pressure when they come into contact with each other. However, this pressure varies over time, with little at first but more as the plates sweep over each other. The question then is how this pressure is released with a minimum amount of damage. With respect to institutions, the rules, norms, principles and decision-making processes are the ways in which these pressures are alleviated over time. However, because there is a dependence on the mechanisms of the regime rather than the member-states, the former begins to assert its own dynamic that may, and often does, alter the power capabilities, preferences and interests of the member-states. In turn, the outward behaviour of the regime in question may change.[46]

For Krasner, the first manner in which a regime may take on an increased role is when it is used by weaker actors as a source of power. The resources of these weaker states do not change within the context of the institution, but their ability to influence the norms, rules and decision-making processes does. The outcome is often an increase in the ability of small states to influence larger ones within the context of the institution.[47] While this situation may not occur at the formation of the regime or institution in question, lags, or incongruities, develop between the character-istics of the regime and the interests of the strongest member-state. These lags allow the weaker states to have a greater influence on the norms, rules, principles and decision-making processes of the regime. In turn, the power of these weaker states is augmented, altering the power distribution within the regime.[48] Second, Krasner posits that regimes may be able to alter the power capabilities of certain actors. By facilitating certain patterns of behaviour, roles, norms and decision-making processes, the resources of a particular actor, or actors, may be strengthened or weakened, again altering the balance of power within the regime.[49]

Krasner's position begs an initial question with respect to which member-state is the strongest actor within the confines of the EBRD. Is it the United States, which is the strongest single actor but which has only 10 per cent of the voting shares, or the member-states of the EU, which as a collective form the strongest actor with a total voting shares exceeding 50 per cent? Different answers to this question will yield different calculations of the interests, resources, capabilities and ability to influence the decisions of the institution on the part of both actors. Given that many of the operating guidelines of the EBRD were codified because of US wants, one might conclude that the United States was the strongest member of the institution at the outset. However, given that the EC and the EIB were accorded member-ship rights, and that the United States was not initially in favour of the very establishment of the EBRD but agreed to it in the end, the alternative position could be taken. However, the original position may again be taken given that most of the recent changes at the EBRD have accorded more with the interests of the US government than those of the EU countries. Also, the possibility that these changes have occurred because of lags and incongruities strengthens Krasner's perspective concerning institutional change and the autonomous nature of regimes. While the epistemic communities of Peter Haas are not accounted for, this approach may offer a more realistic explanation of why changes have occurred at the EBRD over the past three years of operation.[50]

Three approaches

Above is found a description of three theoretically different approaches to understanding how and why states cooperate.

The first approach takes the position that states cooperate
because of the way in which information and knowledge are
presented to them by like-minded knowledge-based experts
who form epistemic communities. These communities are able
to shape the way in which information is presented and therefore
perceived, thus enabling the positions of states to be altered
accordingly. Second, theorists operating from a realist/game
theoretic perspective are of the position that states, operating in
an anarchical setting, cooperate for very self-interested reasons
based upon an assumption of rationality and logic. The points of
cooperation occur within a limited context, those being iterated
scenarios where the 'shadow of the future' is understood to be
present by one or both actors. However, the stag hunt, chicken
and prisoner's dilemma, all of which are situations where
defection is logical within the context of a non-iterated scenario,
are assumed to be the natural choices of primary actors if the
'shadow of the future' is not present. This position takes for
granted actor preferences and brings to this discussion a very
restrictive notion of the role that institutions play in the
determination of state preferences. Instead, it is the international
environment that dominates the decision-making preferences of
these actors.[51] Last, one is presented with a third position, which
is that institutions and regimes are important forces in international relations and, under certain conditions, are able to assist
in changing the preferences, positions and decisions of states.
This position also articulates a belief that, over time, regimes and
institutions produce a dynamic of their own that also may be
able to alter the characteristics and preferences of the same
actors. While the attainment of 'perfect' information is important
in an understanding of why states cooperate to form these
regimes and assist in the development of a growing autonomy
for these institutions, this is not the same as Haas' epistemic
communities. This is so because this knowledge and information

are perceived as 'impartial' rather than subjected to the values, beliefs and preferences of a group of experts.

What really happened

At this juncture, an analysis of what actually occurred at the EBRD will be undertaken, based upon interviews with senior officials who initiated and carried out these changes, representatives of the member-states of the institution and documentation from the latter and the EBRD itself. Finally, the question will be to determine which theoretical explanation of cooperation, if any of the three, appears most relevant in explaining the dramatic changes that have occurred at the EBRD since 1992.

In the immediate wake of the firing of Jacques Attali, the Board of Governors sought to replace him with a person who: had previous experience in the world of international finance and banking; had been involved with an international financial crisis of one sort or another; was acceptable to and comfortable with the United States; would bring to the institution a sense of stability and focus; lacked any grand ambitions for the organization; and was French, so as to allow the French government to save some face in the wake of the Attali debacle. Of the few possible people who met most of these credentials, Jacques De Larosiere appeared to the Board as the person who met all of them. A Frenchmen who was experiencing a distinguished career as an international diplomat at multilateral institutions such as the IMF, he had been involved in finding a solution to the 1982 Mexican debt crisis and was well known for his ability to get along with the leadership of the United States. More importantly, the leadership of the United States was able to get along with De Larosiere. Finally, De Larosiere was not Jacques Attali. A banker by nature without any ambitions to be anything more than that, De Larosiere came to the EBRD with the intention of bringing stability, focus and a new sense of purpose to the organization. Thus he was invited to accept the position of President, which he did.

Soon afterwards, De Larosiere met with senior management and the Board of Directors and the Board of Governors for a weekend to re-establish the aims, goals and mission of the Bank. From this retreat emerged a new, three-pillar approach to project approval, along with a new structural chart for the institution. For any project to approved by the Board of Directors, it would have to meet three new criteria. These were 'sound banking', 'conditionality' and 'transition impact'.[52] With respect to the first, the project in question would have be concluded at a sound rate of return for the EBRD. While not having to guarantee a profit, projects that were expecting not to do so would have a more difficult time before the Board. However, the project would also have to be one that no other type of bank would, or could, finance. Thus the project would have to be risky enough for a merchant bank to be wary of lending its capital. The third condition was that every project would have to have a 'transition impact' upon the country of operation. However, the impact should be, in the final instance, private sector oriented. Thus projects approved would have to illustrate that at some point in time in the near future the company or scheme in question would be transferred from public to private hands. This condition would forever ensure that the original lending requirements of the EBRD would be met.[53]

The second development from this strategic review was the reorganization of staffing. Previously, the EBRD had been divided into two sections – merchant and development – with a senior vice-president for each section. It was decided that this division was not only artificial, given the demands of the countries and businesses in need, but also created a climate of antagonism between the sections, in that they were competing against each other for projects. It was also concluded that there was a lack of accountability and focus in this structure. If a country and business wanted to create a joint venture, both the politician and business person were unsure which section should be approached for assistance at the EBRD. While they could speak to people in various sectoral departments, they were unsure of the rules that defined which projects were merchant and which developmental. Thus deals were either not concluded or were concluded slowly and inefficiently.[54] At first the Board of Directors agreed to a temporary merging of the merchant and development divisions, which would then adopt a north–south division of the regions, but eventually agreed to a country-by-country approach, while maintaining a number of very specific sectoral departments. It has been mentioned that this restructuring has given the EBRD more stability, focus and direction, as well as a more dominant role for those working from a merchant banking background. One reason this has occurred is that Ronald Freeman, the senior vice-president responsible for merchant banking, became responsible for the entire banking division. This left Marcio Sarcinelli, the development vice-president, without a central role in the formulation of banking policy, and those previously working in the development sector of the organization without a natural focal point for decision making other than Freeman.

A third and final development that evolved from the strategic review was the publication of annual *Transition reports* from 1994. These reports are aimed at not only highlighting the work of the EBRD, but also the new principles from which it operates. Rather than being simply an updating of developments in all of the countries of operation and the activities, policies and projects approved of by the Bank, these transition reports are meant to provide an understanding of how, why and by what means the EBRD measures such concepts as 'transition impact'. The *Transition reports* are a means by which, given their language, analysts can note changes in the way the organization does business.

Since the installation of De Larosiere as President, the strategic review and the implementation of its recommendations, the EBRD has, by all accounts, become a more focused, stable and productive institution. People who have been associated with it as clients and as senior management assert that while the EBRD is still slow with respect to project approval and the disbursement of capital, it has improved since the reorganiz- ation.[55] Even its slowness is attributed to the fact that many of the projects it undertakes are 'first projects', which require a tremendous amount of initial research and analysis. This is especially true of projects being approved for Eastern European countries such as the Ukraine, Georgia and Kyrgystan. The time between initial discussions regarding a project and its final approval may be one year, although projects in the more developed countries of Central Europe may now take less than six months to complete.[56]

Learning to cooperate?

Given our knowledge of the history of the EBRD, the questions to be tackled here are threefold. First, have the shareholders of the Bank learned to cooperate? Second, if so, are any of the theories noted above relevant to our attempts to understand this cooperation? Third, if these theories lack relevancy, then what are the theoretical and practical implications of these findings?

The shareholders agree

The EBRD and its shareholders have learned how to cooperate for many reasons and these are based upon aspects of all three theories mentioned above. First, cooperation occurred, in part, out of fear. Shareholders feared that unless some degree of cooperation existed between them, the necessary actions to save the EBRD from international humiliation would not have been taken. A new President and a restructuring of the organization were required, but would not have been instated if this fear had not been present. Second, cooperation also occurred because the shareholders realized that the institution was better placed to act in Central and Eastern Europe than all of them independently and unilaterally. However, the condition imposed for this interdependent cooperation was that the Bank could operate in the future only at a level of the lowest common denominator. The tasks of the EBRD would be changed in such a manner that its scope would be limited to solely those projects that private merchant banks could not or would not finance, that would not guarantee a profitable rate of return and that would have a demonstrable 'transition impact' that would be, at some point in the near future, private sector oriented. Indicative of this position is the definition of 'transition' in the first *Transition report*. The report defined this term as 'the movement towards a new system for the generation and allocation of resources ... [involving] changing and creating institutions, particularly *private* enter-prise'.[57] Therefore cooperation occurred and the institution was revitalized with a new President and a new organizational structure, albeit one that biased one set of ideas concerning the means and aims of 'transition' over another set of ideas, and at the lowest level of agreement that was possible. Had this not occurred at this level – if the EBRD had been allowed to continue to attempt to be ambitious and adventurous in its role in Central and Eastern Europe – cooperation may not have been achieved because those shareholders who had not agreed with the previous direction of the institution might not have agreed to its continuation.

Last, but certainly not least, is the belief that cooperation has been achieved because of the fostering of an epistemic community at the lower levels of the organization. A restructuring of the staff took place that proved helpful in the efficient running of the institution. This restructuring also assisted the formulation of projects because it led to a country-based approach rather than a development/merchant one, and so there was less antagonism between merchant and development bankers. Countries and businesses interested in specific joint ventures are now able to locate a source of information and advice as never before.[58] Previously, there had been a lack of direct communication between the EBRD and the countries in need because of its sectoral and type-of-banking approaches. One might conclude that because of the disappearance of these difficulties, a common voice and position among staff is now able to be heard at the level of senior management and Board of Directors. In turn, this common voice will be able to present project proposals to the Board of Directors that will almost certainly be approved.

The first two reasons for some type and level of cooperation appear to be definitive to a certain extent. Fear concerning the future of the organization coupled with an acknowledgement that the EBRD is useful in its tasks were factors in the establishment of cooperation among differing groups of shareholders. About this there is no doubt, given the comments of senior management and EBRD directors from a variety of countries – both donors and recipients. However, there may be a number of caveats to the third and last theoretical approach to cooperation at the EBRD. The first concerns whether it makes a difference if these organizational changes were led by staff or senior management and the Board of Directors. If it does make a difference, then there is doubt as to the influence that the former had on these changes, which were part of the larger strategic review carried out by senior management and the Board. It appears that this review, while taking into consideration staff concerns, was directed downwards from the Board of Directors and its new President, De Larosiere. The second problem with the 'epistemic community' theory, again related to the strategic review, is that the Board laid down a new three-pillar approach to project proposal acceptance, rather than agreeing to a staff-led approach to the same issue. Relatively few shareholding countries were at the forefront of the creation of the three-pillar approach to proposal acceptance and, as has been mentioned, it took well over a year after the new guidelines were introduced for staff previously situated in the development section of the EBRD to start to feel comfortable with these criteria.[59]

A third caveat is one that reintroduces an old argument – the need to restructure large enterprises prior to their privatization. By and large, EBRD staff were in favour of the position held by Attali, that a number of sectors of the economies of Central and Eastern Europe, as well as Russia, were in such a condition that immediate privatization was not an option. What was suggested in a number of in-house policy papers was the restructuring of these enterprises so that they would become more attractive to private investors, and then privatized. It was thought that it would be almost impossible to accomplish the latter goal without the former.[60] The US Secretary to the Treasury, Nicholas Brady, along with a number of other governors of the EBRD, rejected this approach when it was suggested by Attali at the second annual meeting of the institution.[61] Thus an 'epistemic community' already existed at the institution on an issue of importance, yet cooperation at the senior level of management, with Board of Directors and Board of Governors, was not forthcoming. The identical situation exists in the post Attali era as well. Officials from Anglo-Saxon and continental European countries remain wedded to differing positions on this issue.[62] This continuing difference of opinion lends credence to the strategic review and reorganization of staff duties and priorities being top-down rather than bottom-up processes. It also devalues, to a certain extent, the 'epistemic community' approach itself.[63] Nonetheless, it would not be correct to state that organizational changes did not make possible a more integrated climate at the EBRD among lower-level staff. In turn, these changes have created an environment in which more and better project proposals can be worked on, agreed to and finalized prior to being sent to the Board of Directors.

It would appear that cooperation has taken root at the EBRD because of a combination of all three theories mentioned previously. This initial answer to the original question concerning the state of the EBRD appears to illustrate that no one theory is comprehensively able to explain this type of cooperation. What may be required is either a strengthening of one, if not all three, of these approaches or the development of a new, richer and more comprehensive understanding of international and multilateral cooperation.

Superficial cooperation and its implications

A more detailed analysis of the present state of the EBRD might indicate that another answer is required. The fact that the issue of restructuring/privatization has resurfaced as a point of contention between Anglo-Saxon and continental European shareholding countries may indicate that what has taken place at the EBRD is not cooperation but benign neglect on the part of the latter countries. Another reason for this position may be that countries such as the United States and the United Kingdom have very little reason to be uncooperative and continental European countries such as France have too much to lose by being as uncooperative now as the United States was previously. First, the state of Central Europe is such that there are more small and middle-sized enterprises now than ever before, certainly in comparison with the first two years of the operations of the EBRD. Because of this presence, there are more opportunities for private sector oriented projects and the original mandate of the institution is more than being met. At present, the EBRD is meeting the requirement that 60 per cent of its projects must be private sector oriented. Staff at the institution further stressed that in the 1995 fiscal year, two-thirds of the EBRD's projects were private sector oriented, and many directors believed that this figure would increase even further in countries such as Poland, Hungary, Bulgaria and the Czech Republic.[64] The same pattern will, over time, occur in Eastern Europe and the former Soviet Union as the entrepreneurial spirit takes root and small and middle-sized enterprises develop. Thus a country such as the United States can be as cooperative as it wishes, because the institution in question is, finally, developing in the manner it was originally intended for. This is apparent from the prioritization of the goals of the new three-pillar approach. With the notion of 'sound banking' being the first condition of an EBRD project and conditionality being second, countries such as the United States that demanded that the articles of the EBRD firmly commit the shareholders to a private sector first policy are witnessing the triumph of these original demands. If the argument was not won, it was at least close to being so.

Countries such as the United States can also be more cooperative than before if, as a number of directors mentioned, the EBRD is not an 'important' institution any more.[65] The EU, IMF and World Bank have, in some people's opinions, surpassed the EBRD in importance to Central and Eastern Europe. In this case, there is no need for a country such as the United States to be uncooperative. Such a position would be seen as 'poor' in the eyes of its allies and the other shareholders. One can therefore understand the original demands of the United States and its desire to impose a certain logic on the rest of the shareholders. At the time of the creation of the institution, the potential for the EBRD to affect the transition of the CEECs was still there. However, with other institutions coming to the fore and bringing with them more capital and fewer restraints than the EBRD, the latter has been and will continue to be dwarfed. Given this status, the shareholders are unlikely to approve of any further capital increases for the EBRD or extend its remit in a substantial manner unless it is done in a manner agreeable to the United States. Thus, even if the capital allowance of the EBRD is increased, it will be done with a view to an ever-increasing demand on the part of, primarily, the United States to 'privatize' the EBRD and its lending facilities. In turn, and as will be mentioned in chapter 6, the EBRD will become, over time, an even less important institution, with even fewer reasons for once uncooperative countries to be uncooperative again.

For evidence of the growing 'unimportance' of the EBRD, one can look at the relative importance of EBRD funds in relation to overall foreign direct investment. The latter, for the period 1989–94, was $13.46 billion. EBRD loans for the same period totalled $3.6 billion, or 27 per cent of the total. While the dollars lent by the EBRD continue to rise, they do not maintain the same percentage level with respect to the former figure. It appears that EBRD lending is being restrained *intentionally*, while foreign investment is not.[66] This point is even more interesting given the agreement to double the capital base of the EBRD at the 1996 annual general meeting in Sofia.[67] At this meeting, the EBRD was granted a capital increase of 10 billion ECU.[68] However, the implicit terms of this doubling were that the EBRD would have to 'privatize' more of its lending policies and reinforce its policy of 'sound banking'. In an interview, De Larosiere made the point that the EBRD was, as almost a condition of the capital increase, going to have to assure its more private sector oriented shareholding countries that it was demanding 'sustainable profitability'. This 'deal' between the management of the EBRD and the pro-privatization countries, such as the United States and the United Kingdom (i.e. the Anglo-Saxon countries), mirrors the debates concerning the capital increase of the World Bank/IFC in 1991, as highlighted in chapter 2. There, a capital increase was awarded, but again only after the World Bank/IFC agreed to shift its lending policies from a balance of 'public' and 'private' towards 'private'. Thus commentators in favour of the 'development' aspect of the EBRD were not too pleased with the capital increase, given the trade-off that had to be agreed in return. One such official commented that these restrictions would hinder the transition process, even in the more developed countries of Central Europe. It was asserted that because of the still high level of risk associated with CEEC investments, it 'is hard [even in the Czech Republic] to get equity finance and long-term finance'. Because of this difficulty, the EBRD still has an important role to play because 'it will take time to develop strong Czech corporate governance'.[69]

For countries such as France, which had believed that the EBRD was the start of something significant for the whole of Europe, to be uncooperative would be admit that the argument had been lost. It would also be a sign of admission that the EBRD was not only no longer the type of institution it wanted it to be, but also one that had become dominated by the United States and other Anglo-Saxon countries such as the United Kingdom and Canada, rather than those from continental Europe. While the new President of the EBRD remains French, which was an issue of importance at the outset of the establishment of the institution, he is hardly French in the mould of Attali and Mitterrand. Rather, he appears more Chirac-like in his approach to business. Therefore, what outsiders are witnessing at the EBRD is not a sense of mutual and interdependent cooperation, but a gradual loss of power by one set of countries and the gain of such power by another group of countries. More importantly, the former set of countries is not in a position to be uncooperative, thus creating the appearance of cooperation.

The implications of these findings are interesting and could be far reaching with respect to the institutionalization of interests and the theoretical explanation of institutional formulation and analysis. A first implication is that there remains a role for ideas at the EBRD. The broad and very vague wording of the *Transition reports* in both 1994 and 1995 indicate that there are still disagreements over the type of economic model that should be implemented in Central and Eastern Europe, not to mention the countries of the former Soviet Union, which are still in the earliest stages of their transition. There are a number of examples of this continuing disagreement. A prime example of this wording is in the 1994 *Transition report*'s definition of the ingredients of transition. When speaking of the 'market' the report states that 'it is fundamental to an understanding of the market economy to recognise that the role of the state is not eliminated ... but is transformed'.[70] The implication of this statement is that the 'production of goods and services in the market economy will usually be far from 100 percent in the private sector'.[71]

Second, the fact that the new three-pillar approach is very similar to the initial articles of the institution also illustrates that a divide on the issue of private/public (merchant/development) orientation for the EBRD remains. The adherence to projects that have to meet sound banking *and* conditionality criteria, as well as the hazy notion of 'transition impact', illustrate that the shareholders held a strategic review of the operations of the institution and agreed to disagree. They agreed that differences with respect to economic models and beliefs would remain. One example of this point of contention is the address by Ann Wibble, the chair of the Board of Governors, to the 1994 annual meeting. In her statement, Wibble commented that:

as long as the Bank can demonstrate effectiveness and maintain financial viability, I can endorse a more gradual process towards profitability ... the Bank's profitability should not be a target per se. The real dividends of the EBRD will be flourishing private sectors in the countries it serves.[72]

This speech is juxtaposed by the many remarks by other governors and De Larosiere concerning the need for the EBRD to be more profitable in the ensuing years of operation. Lawrence Summers' allusion to the ability of the United States to repay its wartime debt and produce a balanced budget and De Larosiere's stressing of the financial performance of the EBRD and return on its investment were but further illustrations of this difference of opinion with that of Ann Wibble.[73] What is apparent from the above is that the shareholders did not cooperate enough with respect to the establishment of one set of principles that would act as the future compass of the institution. Because of this lack of cooperation, the EBRD will continue to be surpassed as an instrument to promote transition in Central and Eastern Europe by institutions whose member-states have come to such an agreement, by mutual consent or otherwise.

Do not ask, do not receive

A final initial implication of the above analysis may be that, given the history and present state of the EBRD, one should not ask for what cannot be delivered. Because of how, why and when the EBRD was created, and the span of time taken to do so, academics may be being too high minded in trying to impose upon this institution what it may never have – a clear set of distinct, workable and manageable operational principles. The IMF and World Bank were created and dominated by the United States and the United Kingdom. The EU was created and dominated by France and Germany. All of these institutions were well thought out and established over a period of time when other solutions to economic and capital crises were available. With respect to the IMF and World Bank, neither were actually needed in the immediate post-war period because the United States funded Western Europe through the Marshall Plan and other related programmes. The EC was created in 1958, thirteen years after the end of World War Two, because the original six member-states were already engaged in a series of cooperative political and economic schemes, the OEEC being one example. But in the immediate post-Berlin Wall world, nothing of the kind was on offer save for the EBRD. While individual countries, the EU and the G-24 had initiated a series of transition-related programmes, none was deemed sufficient given the immediate and overwhelming needs of Central and Eastern Europe. Thus the idea of the EBRD was proposed by Mitterrand and accepted in a very short period by over fifty countries. Therefore the principles that would govern the institution were not thought out over a long gestation period, but almost overnight, giving rise to ideas-based disagreements between the shareholders. Given this history, it is no wonder that the EBRD remains plagued by ideas-based differences. Given that the crisis in Central and Eastern Europe still exists, and will continue to do so for the foreseeable future, the EBRD will for that period be an organization unable to 'catch its breath'. It will also be an organization condemned to ideas-based divergences because of the constant need for its services.

Conclusions

What does the above indicate with respect to the utility of the three theories, mentioned at the outset of this chapter, that attempt to say something about cooperation among states?

Because cooperation, at least at a superficial level, has existed between the shareholders for a number of reasons, all of these theoretical positions can be deemed relevant. The question is whether one of them is more relevant than the others – or are they all relevant, but equally lacking in much relevancy?

Donald Puchala mentioned in a 1972 article on theories of integration and the EC that a number of theories attempted to explain the integration process of the EC, but all of them shared a common flaw. This flaw was that, like a blind man, each position believed that the part of the animal it was describing was the entirety of the beast. The problem was that each theory was, in truth, describing only the part of the animal that it was 'feeling' rather than the whole elephant, as their advocates originally thought.[74] The same may be true of the above-mentioned theories concerning cooperation between states. Each of them – the realist, complex interdependent and 'epistemic' models – is able to explain one aspect of cooperation between the shareholding states. However, their collective problem is twofold. The first is that each theory is assumed to able to explain the entirety of cooperation. The second is that even if these theories were combined, they would still not be able to explain the cooperation that has occurred at the EBRD. This is so because what all of them lack is an understanding of 'ideas' and the inhibiting manner that they play with respect to cooperation. Thus what may be required is a theory to explain cooperation that is inclusive of 'ideas' alongside interest-based factors that are present in the theories mentioned above. This will be the task of the next chapter – to carry on from these theoretical findings and explore, in greater detail, an alternative paradigm that may be better able to explain European–US disagreements, as well as cooperation, at the EBRD.

Notes

1 'Growing pains at the EuroBank', *The Economist*, 28 March 1992, pp. 107–8.

2 'Plenty of money but few deals', *EuroMoney*, April 1993, p. 86.

3 EBRD, Information Office press release, 31 July 1995.

4 'Growing pains at the EuroBank', *The Economist*, 28 March 1992, p. 107.

5 *Ibid.*

6 *The Times*, 14 April 1991, p. 1.

7 'Plenty of money but few deals', *EuroMoney*, April 1993, p. 87.

8 *Ibid.*

9 P. Haas, 'Introduction: knowledge, power and international policy co-ordination', *International Organization*, Vol. 46, No. 1, 1992.

10 *Ibid.*

11 *Ibid.*, p. 3.

12 *Ibid.* Later on in the same article Haas simplifies this definition by stating that an epistemic community can be defined as a 'concrete collection of individuals who share the same world view (episteme) and in particular share the four aspects of it that were outlined earlier' (p. 27).

13 *Ibid.*, pp. 16–20.

14 *Ibid.*, p. 19.

15 *Ibid.*, p. 7.

16 *Ibid.*, p. 3.

17 *Ibid.*, p. 5.

18 P. Haas, 'Conclusion: epistemic communities, world order, and the creation of a reflective research program', *International Organization*, Vol. 46, No. 1, 1992, pp. 375–87.

19 See a special issue on epistemic communities in *International Organization*, Vol. 46, No. 1, 1992, especially pp. 375–87.

20 Haas, 'Conclusion', p. 367.

21 *Ibid.*, pp. 368–9.

22 *Ibid.*, pp. 369–70.

23 *Ibid.*, p. 370.

24 See R. Keohane, 'Theory of world politics', in R. Keohane (ed.), *Neorealism and its critics*, New York: Columbia University Press, 1986, pp. 164–8.

25 K. Oye, 'Explaining cooperation under anarchy', *World Politics*, Vol. 38, No. 1, 1985, pp. 6–9.

26 *Ibid.*, pp. 9–14.

27 For a more detailed comment on the 'shadow of the future' and prisoner's dilemma, see R. Axelrod, *The evolution of cooperation*, New York: Basic Books, 1984.

28 R. Jervis, 'Realism, game theory and cooperation', *World Politics*, Vol. 40, No. 3, 1988, pp. 324–8.

29 *Ibid.*, p. 327.

30 *Ibid.*, pp. 336–41.

31 *Ibid.*, p. 340.

32 *Ibid.*, p. 341.

33 J. Mearsheimer, 'A realist reply', *International Organization*, Vol. 20, No. 1, 1995, p. 82. For a more detailed position see Mearsheimer's article 'The false promise of international institutions', *International Security*, Vol. 19, No. 4, 1994/5.

34 Mearsheimer, 'Realist reply'.

35 *Ibid.*

36 *Ibid.*, pp. 86–7.

37 *Ibid.*, p. 87.

38 Of the various works that make these points, see those of Robert Keohane, which include R. Keohane, *After hegemony: cooperation and discord in the world political economy*, Princeton: Princeton University Press, 1984, and R. Keohane and J. Nye, *Power and interdependence*, Boston: Little, Brown, 1977.

39 An institution such as the EBRD would be an example of a formal arrangement between states, whereas a regime would be an example of an informal arrangement between states. However, while an informal arrangement would be a regime and not an institution, a formal arrangement will be a regime as well as an institution. Therefore the two terms – institution and regime – will be used interchangeably here.

40 R. Keohane, *International institutions and state power*, Boulder: Westview Press, 1988, pp. 110–17.

41 R. Keohane and L. Martin, 'The promise of institutional theory', *International Security*, Vol. 20, No. 1, 1995; Mearsheimer, 'Realist reply'.

42 Keohane and Martin, 'Promise of institutional theory', pp. 41–2.

43 *Ibid.*

44 *Ibid.*, pp. 42–6.

45 *Ibid.*, p. 50.

46 S. Krasner, 'Regimes and the limits of realism: regimes as autonomous variables', *International Organization*, Vol. 36, No. 2, 1982, pp. 499–503.

47 *Ibid.*, p. 506.

48 *Ibid.*

49 *Ibid.*, p. 507.

50 See also R. Keohane, 'Achieving cooperation under anarchy: strategies and institutions', *World Politics*, Vol. 38, No. 1, 1985. Keohane stresses, like Krasner, that mutuality of interest, a longer the shadow of the future, a greater number of actors involved and an ability to link the success of one issue to another all increase the opportunity for cooperation, even under anarchic conditions (pp. 228–49). With respect to the shadow of the future, the presence of a long time horizon and the knowledge that both actors will

have to work with each other over a long time will enhance cooperation. This may be so because each state will come to understand and predict the other, primarily through greater access to information and an increased number of contact hours. If more actors exist, the ability to locate and punish defectors decreases and the need to cooperate in the wake of this ability rises. If weaker states are able to link one issue to another that is more important to the stronger actors, then again the potential for cooperation increases. Finally, a mutuality of interest may develop because of changing interests and preferences, changes that have occurred, in part, through greater access to information, a longer shadow of the future and regularity of meetings.

51 For the current debate on the promise of institutions and their ability to influence the decisions of primary actors (states), see the literature and correspondence in *International Security*, Vol. 19, No. 4, 1994 and Vol. 20, No. 1, 1995, in particular the articles by John Mearsheimer, Robert Keohane and, for a critical theoretical perspective, Alexander Wendt.

52 Personal interviews with senior management of the EBRD, January 1996.

53 See De Larosiere's comments in his Per Jacobsen lecture, EBRD, 29 September 1996. He reiterates the same conditions for not only the EBRD, but other multilateral development banks that have to operate in a world of private capital flows.

54 Personal interviews, January 1996. See also comments in the *Proceedings of the third annual meeting of the Board of Governors*, 18–19 April 1994.

55 Personal interviews, January 1996. See also various comments in *Proceedings of the annual meeting of the Board of Governors*, 18–19 April 1995.

56 Personal interviews, January 1996.

57 EBRD, *Transition report*, 1994, p. 4. Another telling comment with respect to the cooperation of countries such as the United States can be found in the text of the US governor's speech at the 1995 annual meeting. Lawrence Summers asserted at the end of his speech that the 'EBRD's role as a public institution will be temporary ... it should [in the near future] consider how to privatize itself'. *Proceedings of the annual meeting of the Board of Governors*, 18–19 April 1995, p. 146.

58 Personal interviews, January 1996.

59 *Ibid*. The notion that other structures inhibit the usefulness of a lower-level epistemic community is inherent in the work of Risse-Kappen. He argues that after an examination of various European powers and their acceptance of Gorbachev's 'new thinking' it is clear that domestic structures should be viewed as intervening variables. Thus no matter how strong the epistemic community may be, there are always going to be hindrances to the fulfilment of the interests of this community. See T. Risse-Kappen, 'Ideas do not float freely', *International Organization*, Vol. 48, No. 2, 1994, pp. 185–214, especially pp. 212–14.

60 EBRD, *Blueprint*, 12 May 1992, p. 5.

61 'Brady attacks ambitions of EBRD', *The Times*, 14 April 1991, p. 1.

62 Personal interviews, January 1996. See also the comments of the US governor, who asserted that the EBRD 'must support aggressive and mass privatisation programmes'. *Proceedings of the annual meeting of the Board of Governors*, 18–19 April 1995, p. 145.

63 It must be said that some of the recent research supporting the 'epistemic community' approach appears to contain similar flaws. Sarah Mendelson asserts that the Soviet withdrawal from Afghanistan was because of the creation of such a community. However, it is apparent from her work that this community was implanted into the Soviet system by Gorbachev. Thus the community did not evolve naturally, but was created. She claims that 'Afghan specialists [supporting withdrawal] served mainly to bolster a position that had been urged by the top echelon for some time'. S. Mendelson, 'Internal battles and external wars', *World Politics*, Vol. 45, No. 3, 1993, p. 259.

64 It must be noted that US and UK officials stress the point that they perceive projects that are 'developmental' in nature private sector oriented if a by-product of such a project will assist a private venture. This is also a key point to the notion of 'transition impact', as mentioned earlier. Recent data confirm that the vast majority of projects being assisted by the EBRD are now private oriented. However, this is no surprise, since the Bank and other organizations have assisted in the development of this sector through both private and public sector loans and co-venture deals. This is exactly why West European directors did not want to establish a lending criterion in the beginning, because the trend towards the private sector has developed as the sector itself has grown.

65 Personal interviews, January 1996. De Larosiere stated in his address to the 1994 annual meeting that 'what is at stake is nothing less than the reintegration of the countries of the region [Central and Eastern Europe] into Europe and the world economy'. *Proceedings of the annual meeting*, 18–19 April 1994, p. 30. However, this appears to be slightly less ambitious than the statement by Mitterrand at the opening of the institution, when he asserted that the creation of the EBRD was one step towards the development of a 'great Europe'. *FT*, 16 April 1990, p. 1.

66 See EBRD, *Transition report*, 1995, for details. See also P. Bod, 'Financing transition in Central and Eastern Europe: the role of the EBRD in the reconstruction of the region', unpublished EBRD memo, 1996. In this memo Bod, a member of the EBRD Board of Governors, concludes that 'the level of the EBRD's activity will be limited by the size of its capital stock, unless the shareholders decide to increase its share capital' (p. 10). However, after conversations with Mr Bod, this author contests that when he speaks of the

need for a capital increase, it is one that is 'real', and not weighed down with private sector oriented restrictions.

67 'EBRD's capital base to be doubled', *FT*, 16 April 1996, p. 2.

68 The 'real' capital increase was only 2.25 billion ECU. The rest, 7.75 billion ECU, was made available to the EBRD through 'callable shares' – guarantees by governments that will allow the EBRD to borrow on the international capital market. Of course, this borrowing came at a price, which would not have been the case had the governments actually given the required amount to the EBRD. Thus this 10 billion ECU was more theoretical than actual.

69 'EBRD's capital base to be doubled', *FT*, 16 April 1996, p. 2.

70 EBRD, *Transition report*, 1994, p. 6.

71 *Ibid*.

72 EBRD, *Proceedings of the annual meeting*, 18–19 April 1994, p. 16.

73 See the statement of De Larosiere in the EBRD, *Proceedings of the annual meeting*, 10–11 April, 1995, p. 31. Under the heading of the EBRD becoming a more effective and efficient organization, the first subheading was the internal financial effectiveness of the institution and its ability to generate a profit. See also speech by Lawrence Summers in the same volume of the *Proceedings*.

74 D. Puchala, 'Of blind men, elephants and internal integration', *Journal of Common Market Studies*, Vol. 10, No. 3, 1972.

5

Foretelling the future?

Introduction

The previous chapters have shown that traditional/mainstream approaches to international relations are unable fully to explain EU–US disagreements within the context of the EBRD. An alternative approach may therefore afford a better and richer understanding of EU–US political economic relations, such as those within the context of the EBRD. This chapter illustrates such an alternative approach to both the initial phases of the establishment of the EBRD and its post-1992 era. This approach is able to lend insights into the nature of cooperation and to take into account the role played by 'ideas' such as collective social images, values and beliefs. The final chapter will then be able to make a number of concluding remarks concerning not only the practical implications of this study, but those of a theoretical nature as well.

An alternative approach to cooperation

Peter Haas asserts that 'the range and impact that we might expect of epistemic-like communities remains conditioned and bounded by international and national structural realities'.[1] How, then, can John Mearsheimer posit, as illustrated in the previous chapter, that these epistemic communities are similar to and should be grouped with perspectives of a critical theoretical nature? Mearsheimer does so on the basis of two overall themes. The first is that, like critical theory, work on epistemic communities is unable to explain why certain discourses rise and others fall. To wit, he also contends there is a similarity because of their inability to explain change in the international system. He cites the work of Thomas Risse-Kappen to make the link between the pitfalls of epistemic community approaches and those of a critical theoretical nature. Second, Mearsheimer compounds this similarity through his belief that 'institutions are at the core of critical theory'.[2] However, the author's attempt to 'institutionalize' critical theory and therefore force a union with work on epistemic communities becomes untenable after the recognition of his own inconsistent logic. Some paragraphs later Mearsheimer claims that critical theory 'assumes that ideas and discourse are the driving forces that shape the world'.[3] Either institutions *or* ideas are the primary interests of critical theorists, but Mearsheimer cannot have it both ways. He cannot at one moment place critical theoretical paradigms alongside those associated with epistemic communities while simultaneously divorcing the two from each other. Save for one reference to the work of Haas and his epistemic community colleagues, the remainder of his attack of critical theory concerns the work of Cox, Ashley and Wendt. None of these academics would place themselves within a group of scholars working on epistemic communities, so why should one take the word of Mearsheimer, especially after the uncovering of these inconsistencies? Thus an independent examination of critical theories approaches is required, with a view to their applicability in comprehensively understanding the political economic transition of Central Europe and the role of the EBRD.

Turning critical

Mark Neufeld stresses that there are two main variants of critical theory in international relations. The first is the Gramscian-inspired neo-Marxist position of Robert Cox and the second is the postmodernism of, for example, Richard Ashley and Rob Walker. Both, for Neufeld, are 'critical' insofar as they are reflexive in their thinking on international relations. Reflexivity, in this instance, is defined in general terms as 'reflection on the process of theorizing'.[4] A more specific definition would be that there are three constituent elements to this process of theorization. These elements are:

1 self-awareness about underlying premises;
2 the denial of the existence of objective standards for assessing competing knowledge claims;
3 the affirmation that reasoned judgements are possible in the absence of a neutral observation language.[5]

For Neufeld, positivist-based theories, such as those mentioned above, including Haas' epistemic community paradigm, are illustrations of perspectives that are not reflexive in their thinking about international relations. In turn, this lack of reflexivity disallows the proponents of these theories from questioning the system in which they operate from a critical perspective. These theorists may argue or contend that a part of the system is not working properly or could be better understood by examining another or different factor, but for Neufeld these are debates at the margins. There is an absence of a questioning not of the parts of the system, but the system itself. Only reflexive theories such as postmodernism or Gramscian-based perspectives, at present, are able to question the system in its totality. This is because these paradigms are, at best, marginal with respect to the system. They are, therefore, able to evaluate critically what they are not part of because they are not products of the system. Thus their continued existence is not dependent upon the maintenance of the system in question. Robert Cox, speaking of his approach, states that he can be critical because his is an approach that 'stands apart from the prevailing order of the world and asks how that order came about'.[6] The same is true of postmodernist international relations theories.

However, of these two critical approaches – the Gramscian and the postmodern – Neufeld suggests that one may be more useful than the other. Cox believes that a theory can be incommensurable without being incomparable. This stance allows one to compare his critical approach with positivistic or problem-solving ones such as neorealist, complex interdependence or the epistemic model of Haas. On the other hand, postmodernists, because of the nature of their project, stand clearly on the side of incommensurable *and* incomparable. This being the case, postmodernism, while interesting as a project, is not as useful if one's goal is to ascertain which theoretical position is able to contribute to a richer and more comprehensive understanding of a given subject.[7] With respect to this project, the goal is to ascertain why and how countries cooperate. Given that the previously mentioned theories are unable to explain this fully, one must not only utilize an alternative perspective, but in some manner compare this latter stance with those previously examined. An incommensurable and incomparable stance disallows this author to do so, invalidating the usefulness of the postmodern project.[8] We are left with, but not to our detriment, the Gramscian-inspired critical theoretical approach to international relations of Robert Cox. What is most relevant for this project is not only Cox's inclusiveness of ideas in the calculation of interest, but also his interpretation of Gramsci's concept of hegemony, which of course is very much pertinent to international relations.

Throughout his work, Cox speaks of the need to think critically rather than in a problem-solving manner. However, he also speaks of the need to rethink our conception of hegemony and of how this position of dominance is attained domestically, regionally, internationally or within the confines of an institution such as the EBRD. Rather than a Weberian 'power over', hegemony is defined by Gramsci as 'the permeation *throughout* civil society … of an entire system of values, attitudes, beliefs, morality'.[9] This definition strongly suggests that the construction of a new order is through 'ideological domination rather than direct political coercion'. This stance gives rise to Cox's position that the creation of a new order in any society is brought about by establishment of:

> reciprocal relationships of the political, ethical and ideological spheres of activity with the economic sphere … [and therefore] ideas and material condition are always bound together, mutually influencing one another, and not reducible one to another.[10]

Rather than giving priority to one set of factors or another, this definition of the process through which hegemony is attained speaks of a partnership between ideas and material capabilities, of consensus and coercion, of politics, economics and belief systems. Cox stresses this point when he asserts that hegemony must be seen as a 'fit between power, ideas and institutions'.[11] If this position is taken, it is becomes possible to 'deal with some of the problems in the theory of state dominance … [and] allows for lags and leads in hegemony'.[12]

This paradigm takes on board and deals with not only those issues thought to be the preserve of neorealism, but also the institutionalism of complex interdependence and the lags and incongruities spoken of by Stephen Krasner (see chapter 4).

Because of this inclusiveness, while remaining critical and reflexive in its essence, the Coxian analysis of Gramsci may be able to do what three other approaches have been unable to accomplish to date – the production of a richer and more comprehensive analysis of member-state cooperation at the EBRD. Nonetheless, there are issues to be dealt with concerning the applicability of the Gramscian approach. These include comments by Nicholas Rengger, Mearsheimer, Randall Germain and Michael Kenny, and Peter Burnham.

Rengger's foundationalism

In the article which spurred Rengger to comment on the utility of the Coxian Gramscian project, Mark Hoffman spoke of the crossroads at which the discipline of international relations was coming to in the mid to late 1980s. The appearance of a number of pieces stemming from an alternative and primarily critical theoretical vantage point was, for the author, the beginning of a new and serious challenge to the position accorded traditional theories of international relations.[13] Hoffman instituted this debate by retelling the story of critical theory via the development of the Frankfurt School and the work of Horkheimer, Adorno, Marcuse, Fromm and Habermas. He contended that this school of thought was 'not merely an expression of concrete realities of the historical situation, but also a force for change within those conditions'.[14] To this end, the Frankfurt School developed a relationship with Marxism, but with the belief that the latter needed to become less deterministic and mechanistic in order for it to develop into a 'critical' paradigm. Therefore an uneasy relationship developed between the two approaches over time.

Two types of critical theory regarding international relations developed from these foundations. The first is exemplified by Richard Ashley's response to Ken Waltz's book *Theory of international politics*,[15] and the second is Robert Cox's rejoinder to the same work. Both, along with the relevant chapters of Waltz's work, are to be found in a book edited by Keohane, *Neorealism and its critics*.[16] For Hoffmann, Cox's rejoinder is the more important of the two. Hoffman's discussion of nature, the subjectivity of theory and the relationship that exists between interest and knowledge and reliance on 'ideas' and those forces that contribute to a more comprehensive understanding of institutions and material capabilities provide the link needed to associate the Frankfurt School and critical theory with Marxism.[17] Hoffman then sets out what he considers the seven main points of this approach,[18] and compares and contrasts other so-called alternative approaches to international relations with this set of conditions. To this end, both the world order models project of Richard Falk and Johan Galtung, as well as the world society approach of Burton, fall short of what Hoffman believes Cox would call a 'critical' theoretical approach to politics. For many of the same reasons, even Ashley's work is found lacking because it is not emancipatory and does not contain a new set of ordering principles or a sense of self-realization or reflexivity.[19] Thus what is left standing alone as part of the 'new' inter-paradigm debate, for Hoffman, is the Coxian approach to international relations via the use of the Gramscian approach to Marxism, which is not based on international relations. Therefore while Hoffman contends that critical theory represents the 'next stage' in the development of international relations theory, he is really speaking about how Cox's version of critical theory (in 1987) represents this next stage.

In response to this argument, Rengger begins by stating that he does agree that the developments being labelled as 'critical theoretical' do represent the next important stage in the study of international relations.[20] The author is explicit in this belief when he says that critical theory 'remains one of the most fruitful areas of potential research open to the theoretically inclined international relations scholar'.[21] However, he does contend that these are early days and that there are points within this approach which for him appear to be problematic. Going back to the seven points laid down by Hoffman that for him encapsulate Cox's approach, Rengger focuses on three. These include Hoffman's belief that Coxian theory:

1 'questions the origins of the legitimacy of social and political institutions ... [and] seeks to define what elements are universal to world order and what elements are historically contingent';

2 contains 'a normative, utopian element, in favour of a social and political order different from the prevailing order, but also recognizes the constraints placed upon possible alternative world orders by historical processes';

3 is 'a guide for strategic action, for bringing about an alternative world order'.[22]

Rengger's claim is that the glue that holds all three of these propositions together is something like the rationalism of Michael Oakeshott. If true, then this would link Cox's Gramscian approach to the very traditional readings of international relations that he seeks to move away from. Oakeshott contests that his rationalism is about problem solving, and what distinguishes Cox from the likes of Waltz in his own mind is that his Gramscism is not a problem-solving theory.[23] Thus to contend that Cox slides back into a problem-solving mode because of an element of rationalism is to contend that he is not at all 'critical' in his approach to international relations. Rengger does so but makes the point that in order to search for an alternative world order, one must have some identifiable criteria through which this new order can be found. To this extent there is a semblance of rationality involved. Oakeshott himself, the critic notes, described those who are rationalists as slightly utopian, interested in the 'Pursuit of the Ideal'.[24] The fourth and sixth contentions of Hoffmann with respect to Cox (points 1 and 2 above), which then invoke the seventh (point 3), speak of this utopian ideal.

With rationalism, then, comes an aspect of foundationalism that ties Cox to the prevailing order – its culture, language, mores, values, beliefs – that he seeks to transcend. However, if Cox does manage to transcend this prevailing order and stand apart from it, then his propositions become 'incommensurable', in that one will be unable to gauge the relative 'betterness' of this world order compared with that which we already operate from.[25] Here is a contradiction. For Cox to develop an alternative world order, he must transcend the prevailing one. However, in order to do so, he must lay down a set of criteria by which one can search for and create this new order. This, in turn, to a certain extent will most likely be done through the use of pre-existing values found within the order Cox seeks to transcend. He must, nonetheless, use these pre-existing values, to some extent, for if he does not then one will lack the means by which to judge the extent to which he has transcended this old order and created an alternative one. But by using existing values one becomes rationalist as well as foundationalist. By being both, one might find it difficult also to be 'critical'. Coxian critical theory, based upon the seven propositions of Hoffman, which stem from his reading of Cox's approach, appear to Rengger as an ever-increasingly entangled web, leading to 'an endless conversation ... of the West'.[26]

Mearsheimer, critical theory and false promises

A second, more recent and traditionalist criticism of the Gramscian position (and in general that of critical international relations theory) is that of John Mearsheimer. In his critique of the ability of international institutions to change state preferences and mitigate the anarchical self-interested power-maximizing nature of the international system, Mearsheimer attacks the positions of those academics who place their faith in the utility of liberal institutionalism, notions of collective security, such as the Concert of Europe and the Congress of Vienna, and critical theorists. In each instance, he lays out what he considers to be the initial and underlying assumptions of these theoretical positions and then notes the 'flaws' in their causal logic with respect to empirical evidence.

To this end, Mearsheimer highlights three central flaws within the critical theoretical argument. The first is that these theorists provide 'few insights on why discourses rise and fall'.[27] With specific reference to the discourse of neorealism, Mearsheimer contends that critical theory cannot and does not explain why it has been the dominant theory and why it is (in his estimation) facing hegemonic challenges in the post-1989 era. He does note that critical theory can point to factors that might lead to a change in international relations discourse, but grudgingly in that this happens 'occasionally', and when it does it is because of changes in material conditions rather than any other forces or factors. Thus, rather than strengthening critical theoretical claims, they weaken them by resorting to the use of 'neorealist' evidence. Mearsheimer cites the work of Richard Ashley from the mid-1980s as a case in point.[28]

A second downfall of critical theory, according to Mearsheimer, is that while it predicts the hegemonic decline of neorealist thinking, it is unable to predict which theoretical traditional model will replace it. This is so because it is a paradigm that 'says little about the direction change takes'.[29] He quotes Cox's comment that utopian expectations are rarely realized in practice as evidence of this failure to predict the future. In light of this,

Mearsheimer concludes that critical theory could be termed 'wishful thinking'.

The third and most damning criticism, and not surprisingly like that of Burnham's open Marxism (see below), is that empirical research fails to match the predictions of critical theory. For example, many critical theorists, Mearsheimer contends, assert that the states of the early state system of Europe did not act in a self-interested manner all of the time, thus illustrating that while the state system has been in operation for almost 700 years, states have not acted as if this system conditioned them to act in a certain manner. The same is true of a critical theoretical interpretation of Gorbachev's Soviet Union, in that many perceive Gorbachev to be a 'critical theoretical leader' by way of his 'new thinking'. Mearsheimer asserts that while lawfulness was an aspect of the early modern state system, so too were war, alliance formations, balances of power, the threat of force and the attempt to build spheres of influence. Similarly, since the downfall of Gorbachev, the Soviet Union/Russia has returned to an offensive military doctrine and relates to many of its neighbours in a classically imperial manner.[30] While not mentioned, the formation of the CIS, with Russia as the core, the bullying of Belarus and its aggressive overtones with respect to NATO enlargement, the Ukraine and the Baltic states appear to be very 'realist/neorealist' in orientation. Thus critical theory may be an interesting heuristic device, but given its inability to predict or posit an alternative, and to match theory with empirical data, it will forever 'remain in realism's shadow'.[31]

The attack from within

A third criticism of the overall Gramscian approach comes via Randall Germain and Michael Kenny. Their general point with respect to how this approach has been applied by numerous scholars is that the latter have 'failed to engage critically with some of the key premises underlying its appropriation of Gramsci'.[32] Beyond this, there are a number of specific comments made. A first is that international relations scholars simply 'apply' Gramsci, rather than understanding the conditions in which his work should and can be applied. The second is that the co-authors are not clear whether or not Gramsci's 'conceptual categories can be meaningfully "internationalized"'.[33] Specifically, they pursue the line that Gramscists are attempting to disembed civil society from the nation-state, yet one of the apparent goals of Gramsci was to comprehend the 'statism' of the twentieth century. Thus Gramscists of today are appearing to go against the project as it was initially conceived.[34]

A first specific concern is with the concept of 'historicism'. The co-authors note that Stephen Gill has partly redefined historicism by stating that historical necessity is about the social interaction and political change that take place within a given social structure, and are therefore not limited. However, a question remains as to the degree to which these possibilities are fixed and unchangeable, or discursively constructed and therefore not limited in scope. To wit, the co-authors claim a static interpretation on the part of Gill with respect to the relationship between the intellectual and the ideological processes on the one hand, and social structures on the other, which assist in either limiting or opening up these possibilities.[35]

The second main issue is that of the 'internationalization' of Gramsci. For the co-authors, the Gramscian notion of civil society was made up of networks of formal and informal institutions and cultural practices 'which mediate between the individual and the state'.[36] If one internationalizes Gramsci, does the state disappear? And if so, where does the notion of civil society come into play? For the authors it is 'difficult to imagine how Gramsci would conceptualize a civil society … [not] considered in relation to the nation-state'.[37] But this is exactly what they claim is occurring within the confines of Gramscians working in the field of international relations. By locating power at the level of transnational institutions such as the IMF, the Trilateral Commission, financial markets, capital or class formations, the state drops out of the picture in the name of 'globalism' or 'internationalism' or 'transnationalism'.

The same is true of the third criticism of contemporary international relations Gramscians. The concept of hegemony is based upon the development of a civil society of a certain kind, but one at the level of the nation-state. Can this type of hegemony be reproduced at the international/global level of politics without the nation-state? For Germain and Kenny, this appears to be difficult and, moreover, appears not to have been addressed by these international relations scholars.[38] They contend that new Gramscians assume that the appearance of a certain type of discourse at the international level indicates the presence of a certain type of global hegemony, and that unit and/or subunit actors attempt to resist this language. It is a one-dimensional perspective, which disengages itself from the possibility, and probability, that these non-global actors may alter the 'terrain' of this language through their resistance, therefore making the relationship two dimensional, if not more.[39]

The authors conclude that the study of international relations will greatly benefit from the critical analysis that Gramscian Marxist thought brings to the subject. However, this will only be so when international relations Gramscians engage in the material in such a way that Gramsci himself is historicized and contextualized, as well as rejected as a deity in himself. Instead, these theorists need to take from Gramsci what is relevant and discard what is not, rather than treating his writings as the be all and end all of critical theoretical work. However, in the process of doing so, we need to be aware of not only what we are using but how, and to be aware of whether we are using it true to the spirit and intent of the original author. Only then can this engagement be useful to the development of a more critical theoretical approach to international relations.

Burnham and open Marxism

The final critique of a Gramscian variant of Marxist thought stems from Burnham's use of 'open Marxism' and its criticism of Gramscism for being pluralist in orientation. This is centred around the main argument that Cox prioritizes 'ideas' and the role of 'organic intellectuals' instead of capital, thus leading to a non-mechanistic interpretation of Marxian thought.

Burnham condemns Cox for offering little more than another version of Weberian pluralism in that this pluralism is defined by an acceptance of the structural variability and historical specificity of data.[40] Cox's adherence to a reciprocal relationship between ideas, institutions and material capabilities appears to match this variability of Weber, insofar as it does not accord 'capital' a leading role. Through wanting to escape the determinism and economies of classical Marxism such as that of Althusser, Cox has placed himself within a 'post-Marxist' camp that is not at all Marxist in orientation. Burnham asks, rhetorically, what 'ideology' has to do with the ways in which capital determines the alienation of humankind.[41]

The author's second attack on Coxian Gramscian is the apparent reliance on 'organic intellectualism'. Burnham points to the work of Gill and Law, who estimate that UK policy with respect to EC in the mid to late 1950s was 'rational' if one fits its material capabilities (foreign direct investment patterns that continued to prioritize the United States and the Commonwealth) to its ideas (Anglo-Saxon chauvinism) and therefore to its domestic institutions (the Foreign Office) and those external institutions the United Kingdom decided to join (EFTA) or not join (the EEC). Instead, Burnham points to an alternative argument that illustrates the incorrectness of the Gill/Law position, in that the United Kingdom was active not only in the United States and the sterling bloc, but also Latin America and Western Europe. He claims that the preference for an Atlantic and Commonwealth trading system had 'little to do with the consciousness of policy makers or the articulation of a persuasive ideology'.[42] Rather, UK choices were conditioned and made because of increasing inter-imperialist rivalry brought about because of the contradictions of capital relations due to uneven development. Thus, for the author, 'ideas' and 'organic intellectualism' may have a place, but not on equal footing with that of 'material capabilities' such as capital.[43]

The third area of criticism for Burnham with respect to Coxian theory relates to the constituent elements of the historic bloc. The bloc is the organic link between structure and superstructure through the medium of a dominant ideology. This ideology is based around a larger, and looser, set of ideas, defined as a set of shared notions of the nature of social relations or as collective images of the social order. For Burnham, this attempt to root Marxist thinking in a set of 'ideas' and/or an ideology 'falls foul ... of a mechanistic interpretation of Marx'.[44] The problem with this type of thinking is that one allocates more time analysing 'beliefs about' rather than the ideological effects of material practices on the subject (the emphasis here on the material practices causing ideological thought rather than the opposite). To this end, when one places the (correct) emphasis on the latter rather than the former type of analysis, two realities appear. The first is that recovery from crisis is inherent in the process of capitalist reproduction, whereas the second is that the systemic integration of capitalism is not dependent on the internationalization of shared norms understood in terms of a dominant ideology.[45]

Burnham's final argument is that Cox seeks to replace the state with a study of class forces in a national/international/transnational context. However, given that the modern political era is rooted in and based on the existence of a state-centric system, even such processes as globalization and the appearance of transnational companies (in contrast to multinational companies) do not take away from the presence and importance of states in the conduct of international relations. For the author, the durability of the nation-state propels us to seek to develop a theory of the international state, which is not what Cox and those working within the prism of Gramscian Marxism are attempting to do. Cox's belief that the state is a 'social construct', rather than some fixed entity that exists in reality, is the basis of Burnham's criticism.[46] Again, this points to Cox's prioritization of 'ideas' over material capabilities, of 'ideology' instead of capital. To this end, Burnham concludes by stating that a Gramscian interpretation of Marxism 'simply offers a pluralist analysis of global capitalism which overemphasises the role of ideology in economic policy and regime formation'.[47]

A rebuttal

What is notable from the above is that Mearsheimer's and Burnham's criticisms, while stemming from almost polar opposite positions on the theoretical spectrum, attack Coxian Gramscian and critical theory in general (more Mearsheimer on this point than Burnham, whose work is directed mainly at Cox) with similar criticisms. What is even more fascinating, at the outset, is that they both denigrate Cox's approach for not being what Rengger thinks it is, which is rationalist/foundationalist in orientation. However, because of some of the implications of Burnham's criticisms, his will be dealt with last.

Rather than refuting some of Mearsheimer's points of contention, it may be more useful to analyse his own argument and the places from which it is derived. Mearsheimer does get it right when he comments that critical theorists take ideas very seriously, in that ideas shape practice.[48] His second point, that this use of ideas stretches only to the point of highlighting contradictions rather than also pointing out alternative futures, is subjective and selective. Mearsheimer quotes from Cox's *Production, power and world order* (1987), rather than from his more recent work, which does ascertain the need for a project and an alternative future.[49] Prior to pointing out the flaws in the causal logic, Mearsheimer describes this logic. It is in this section that Mearsheimer skates on thin theoretical ice. He begins by asserting that 'institutions are at the core of critical theory'.[50] First, is not the complex interdependent approach about formal and non-formal regimes? And second, if ideas are the most important aspect of critical theory, then how can institutions be as well, simultaneously? It would appear that it can only be one, or the other, but not both. And we have just been witness to an attack on Cox's neo-Gramscian analysis because of its prioritization of 'ideas' over everything else, including institutions. Given that Mearsheimer points out how critical theorists are antistructural with regard to Marx because of his 'realist' tendencies,[51] can Burnham and Mearsheimer both be correct, albeit for diametrically opposed reasons, if they both come from structuralist backgrounds?

Mearsheimer can, although he starts from the wrong starting point. He cites institutions as the core elements of critical theory because of his reading of the literature on 'epistemic communities' by scholars such as Adler and Peter Haas. Thus he also derives the contention that critical theory is about the creation of a 'more harmonious and peaceful international system'.[52] Further, he conflates this confusion by incorporating the work of Deutsch with that of Ashley and Wendt, the latter openly admitting to his 'scientific realist' tendencies rather than those of a critical theoretical variety, and John Ruggie, more known for his liberal institutional/regime theorization approach than anything else.[53] Therefore it would appear that the contradictions within Mearsheimer's work on critical theory stem less from his lack of understanding of what critical theory is about and more from whom he conceives as being a critical theorist. Rengger makes the intellectually sensitive point that the theoretical work of Der Derian and Shapiro is critical, but unlike that of Cox, whose work is distinct from that of Ashley.[54] Instead, Mearsheimer lumps all of these so-called critical theorists together along with those who are critical theorists. Worse, while admitting to distinctions among critical theorists, he proceeds not to make or at least to be sensitive to this distinction in his description of the causal logic, even though he admits there is one, by noting that there are post-structuralists, postmodernists, reflectivists and contructivists. It is difficult to take seriously a criticism of a theoretical approach that appears to be as insensitive and (self)misinformed as this one.

Two other points come to light from this (re)reading of Mearsheimer on critical theory. The first of these is that the critical theoretical attack on neorealism is obvious, for this is the paradigm that stands between critical theory (presumably all branches and variations) and hegemonic dominance of the discipline of international relations. Thus critical theorists perceive neorealism as 'dangerous' and are therefore intolerant of it. The question is who is more intolerant of what – the critical theorist who responds to the actual texts of realist thought, or the realist who responds to texts that are not even considered to be slightly 'critical' in orientation? The second point of contention is one that appears to have the more validity for this project. Mearsheimer asserts that what is very problematic with critical theory is the lack of an alternative future. It is a project interested in the possibility of launching social movements rather than focusing on what the movement might, can or did achieve over time. This is so because there is a lack of a fixed point from which critical theory can develop an alternative future. The problem is a lack of determinism and the overwhelming presence of 'no constants, no fixed meanings, no secure grounds, no profound secrets'.[55] And if there is, Mearsheimer would eventually contend that critical theorists lack the ability to explain how to get there.

Last, but certainly not least, are the criticisms of critical theory, and notably the Coxian variant, by Rengger and Kenny and Germain. Here are two positions that are discrete, sensitive and positive. With regard to Rengger's work, the overarching difficulty that the author has with Coxian critical theory is its return to foundationalism and rationalism in spite of its attempt to be neither. In an attempt to 'go beyond' traditional international relations theories, Cox is trapped in the world, and its values, that he wishes to leave. Thus he is not attacked for the want of an alternative world or the prioritization of 'ideas' over capital, but because some of these ideas and some of the constituent elements of that alternative world order are of the old order Cox disagrees with. But to do anything different would be to descend into the problem that Mearsheimer and Burnham, as it will be pointed out below, appeal to – meaningless interpretation which would lack a standard from which one can begin, and compare against other world orders. Cox is, therefore, stuck between two worlds – the world he wishes to get to, and the one he wants to leave – for the same reasons.

On the heels of Rengger's criticisms are those of Kenny and Germain. In all aspects of their paper crucial points are made, not least the one concerning the 'internationalization' of the notion of civil society. There is the concern that people using Gramsci within the world of international political economy believe in the presence of a global civil society – the mafia, central bankers, transnational business elites – that is detached from both the state and nation. These are projects quite dissimilar from this one, save for an interest in being inclusive of the notion of 'civil society' through the use of ideas alongside material capabilities and institutional processes. Kenny and Germain's criticisms appear not to be as relevant to this study because it is, by and large, an examination of differences between nation-states and groups of nation-states rather than actors at the transnational level. There is much in this project that is taken from the EBRD, such as the raw data concerning its activities and the views of EBRD staff who are not working from within a country paradigm, but this information serves as a pointer or confirmation of the views of staff, directors and other people working at the EBRD who are seconded from national institutions. Thus there is no intention of replacing the nation-state with that of a global society. In truth, the politics of transitional assistance cannot be divorced from the actions of the nation-state given the intergovernmental rather than supranational nature of the EBRD. The EBRD, per se, does not have an economic policy of its own divorced from that which its donor countries wish it to have, and it is the very disagreements between nation-states over a global/international transitional policy for Central and Eastern Europe that is the very subject of this book. Therefore if the study is required to speak about what occurs at the level of global politics, it is only in order to understand the agreements and disagreements taking place at the level of the nation-state and between nation-states.

One implication might come out of this, nonetheless. What Kenny and Germain are speaking about are those academics who invoke the name of Gramsci without using what they consider to be key elements of Gramsci's theorization. Hence the question of whether these new Gramscians are what they claim to be. This is relevant to this project because the class/economic elements of Marxist thought that are still to be found in Gramsci's writings are not analysed in this work, because of the strategic nature of the matter. Therefore there is the potential for one to claim that this is not a Gramscian analysis because it uses only certain aspects of this paradigm and not others. To this end, the use of Gramsci's notion of 'civil society' again becomes relevant. It is not enough to say that one is interested in seeking out the 'ideas' aspect of EBRD policy (or the lack thereof) in order to illustrate the contradictions and flaws in these policies. As will be pointed out with respect to Burnham's comments, there are a number of theoretical approaches that allude to and/or speak of 'ideas'. The question is whether or not these other approaches have the same understanding of 'ideas' and their relation to 'civil society' as that of Gramsci (as appropriated by Cox) and how aspects of the process of enlargement match up with these definitions. To meet the demands of Kenny and Germain, one must not only say the words, but also speak the same language and use identical reference points. Otherwise, it is an attempt to be Gramscian without Gramsci.

With respect to Burnham, Bieler has worked to refute the various criticisms levelled by the open Marxist approach.[56] By and large, his arguments rest on a recital of a number of key quotations from Marx and Gramsci's *Prison notebooks* to show that the 'open Marxism' variant of Burnham is not the only variant of Marxism. The point of these textual references is that one is able to read into Marx, along with other Marxian texts, a different type of Marx, which is not deterministic or economistic in orientation. While correct and engaging, this level of argument lends, in this author's opinion, credibility to the Burnham position. Anyone can find a quotation to fit their respective theoretical leanings, and that might be the response of Burnham and the 'open Marxists' to the work of Bieler. The latter might be on stronger ground by making a simple argument in favour of the Coxian Gramscian approach through Burnham's own words.

Throughout the article, Burnham attacks Cox for being Weberian insofar as his is an approach that seeks to go beyond the economism and overdetermination of classical Marxist thought.[57] He further concludes that by taking an 'ideas first' and 'capital second' approach, Cox is 'unwittingly in the post-Marxist camp struggling to escape an economism'.[58] Further, and again with respect to the role of ideas, Burnham comments negatively that a neo-Gramscian paradigm '*necessarily* leads to an overestimation of the importance of ideology'.[59] He plays on this theme again when he states that the result (unfortunately) of a neo-Gramscian approach that strives to be non-economistic is to give equal weight to ideas, institutions and material capabilities, and that by doing so Cox, as mentioned earlier, 'falls foul ... of a mechanistic interpretation of Marx'.[60] Burnham is correct in this assertion. This may be for two reasons. The first is that Gramsci himself falls foul of this type of Marxism, for he does not believe in it. A return to *The prison notebooks* is indicative of this position, for many traditional Marxist terms are defined and used in non-traditional ways. Gramsci is explicit in how he defines human nature and its constituent elements. The former is the 'totality of historically determined social relations'.[61] He takes great pains, from then on, to point out that these relations are objective (structures independent of human will), material (military) and political (self-awareness) in orientation. He further asserts that because all three constitute social relations, it is difficult to establish which one at any given time is more important than the other two.[62] A main implication of this understanding is that one should be neither to economistic nor too ideolistic in orientation, for it is a combination of both that will assist one in the 'posing and resolving question involving the entire subsequent development of national life'.[63]

The above illustrates a lack of deference by Gramsci to a traditional understanding of Marxism.[64] Given this, it is therefore not surprising that neither has Cox in his appropriation of Gramsci's work. And he, too, is explicit in this, not only his work in *Neorealism and its critics* but also in *Power, production and world order*, his first major Gramsci-oriented work. In the former, Cox is explicit in his desire to move away from what he calls problem-solving theories. These, for him, are not only of a realist or neorealist variation, but also a classical Marxist one. This is why Cox is critical of readings of Marx such as that by Althusser.[65] Rather, Cox is adamant about the need to have a theory of the state, like Gramsci himself, albeit while simultaneously taking into account those factors such as ideas, globalization and trans-nationalism that realists and neorealists ignore.[66] The purpose of *Power, production and world order* is to 'consider the power relations in societies and in world politics from the angle of power relations in production'.[67] 'Production' is defined as that which 'creates the material basis for all forms of social existence'.[68] Initially, this would suggest a traditional definition, but on further reading a different interpretation can be found, in that Cox asserts in the first chapter that production can be understood only within the context of the social and political context of the times. Further, each mode of production is 'matched by an intersubjective content – the common understandings shared by the people embraced by the mode in respect to the relationships and purposes in which they are involved'.[69] This is so because the origins of conflict between groups involved in productive relations are to be found outside this relationship in the 'ambient society'. Moreover, production is not only about traditional concerns, such as its allocation, distribution and organization, but also these intersubjective ideas[70] – ethics and rationalities of production – spoken of above, as well as institutions, and the reciprocal nature of these three objective, subjective and institutional factors.[71]

It is because of Cox's understanding of production that Burnham condemns him for overestimating the role of ideas and

ideology. Again, if Cox was attempting to redefine a classical
Marxist tradition in a traditional manner, this criticism may be
valid. Because he is explicitly not, how can he be condemned for
this overestimation? And is it, in fact, an overestimation of ideas
on the part of Cox when his project is to bring into the discussion
of production a set of subjective factors that have been ignored
for a considerable period? Is he overestimating, or simply re-
introducing? For Burnham and other classical Marxists, it appears
that the two are equally reprehensible and no more defensible.
Having said this, there is an important implication stemming
from Burnham's criticisms, coupled with those of Rengger and
Kenny and Germain. This is the 'Gramscian without Gramsci'
argument. If you adopt an approach that leaves aside some of the
aspects of Gramscian Marxism, can it still represent itself as such,
or has it become something else? If one drops from Marxism its
economically deterministic aspects, but is still inclusive of 'ideas',
is one being Gramscian, pluralist or a sophisticated neorealist in
orientation while trying to feign being the first? Given that there
has been some recent work in the area of ideas and foreign policy
by a number of well respected pluralists and neorealists, the
question arises of what separates this work from that of Gramsci
in general and specifically with regard to this case study on the
role of the EBRD in the political economic transition of Central
and Eastern Europe?

Wendt's constructivism

One 'internationalist' claim by a non-Gramscian was made by
Alexander Wendt in his article on 'Collective identity formation
and the international state'.[72] His aim was to bridge the gap
between neorealist and neoliberal thinking with respect to
collective action. Wendt's claim is that in between these two
positions is a constructivist agenda that examines the creation of

identities and interests. This agenda, building upon the inter-subjective nature of the structures of the state system and states themselves as social structures, can assist in the explanation of collective action by states.[73] For Wendt, these intersubjective structures can consist of shared understandings, expectations and social knowledge embedded in international institutions and threat complexes.[74] However, the author assures the reader that space is left for the effects of material capabilities, as is the case with neorealism, while not submitting to a purely materialist notion of political behaviour. Similarly, the introduction of inter-subjective structures is an attempt to move away also from the rationalist notion of these structures as external to behaviour and static. Instead, these structures are endemic to the process of state activity, changing over time because of the context, capabilities and institutional relationships of a state at a given time.

The potential effect of the inclusion of these structures is that through interaction, the identities of a state may be altered in such a manner that collective action is possible. An 'inter-nationalized' state may develop by way of institutionalized cooperation at that level of association. Again, this development assumes that state behaviour is based on not only materialist or domestic political concerns, but also the formation of interests, as identities in a reciprocal manner. As much as the former two act on the latter, the latter impacts on the former. Wendt asserts in his conclusion that 'it is also about the reproduction and trans-formation – by intersubjective dynamics at both the domestic and systemic levels – of the identities and interests through which those incentives [material and rational] and worlds are created'.[75]

Liberalism

Both Risse-Kappen, in a work on cooperation among democratic states, and Keohane and Goldstein, in their co-authored book on ideas and foreign policy, present similar ideas to the above constructivist approach of Wendt. In brief, the former also notes the gaps that exist in understanding cooperation between a variety of democratic states. He asserts that the traditional theories on alliance formation which emphasize strategic interests and power-based bargaining do not provide sufficient answers. For that matter, Risse-Kappen also excludes the hegemonic stability theories of realism because of they do not facilitate an understanding of cooperation.[76] In response to these deficient approaches, the author contends that a theory based on a liberal notion of international relations, coupled with arguments emphasizing the role of norms and communication between states within the context of an institution, is best able to explain relations between small and large democratic states. By focusing on this approach, Risse-Kappen contends that small and large democratic states form a community with a collective identity. Institutional processes such as guidelines for consultation and decision-making/voting rules encourage allied cooperation and establish a framework in which small states gain bargaining power irrespective of the material strengths of their larger allies. The importance of domestic constituencies, bureaucratic actors and the transnational/governmental nature of the development of this power by small states are also noted by the author in the introduction and the four case studies that illustrate his theoretical position.[77]

Risse-Kappen then provides a fuller basis for his case studies, namely the inability of realist theory to account for communitarian values and the ability of liberal international relations to be inclusive of the same factors. The author concludes that democratic states do not tend to go to war with each other because they share values. This tendency is enhanced by the creation of institutions and processes that encourage certain norms of behaviour that emphasize these democratic values and peace. Risse-Kappen argues that, in contrast, non-democratic countries tend to cooperate for narrowly defined self-interested reasons, and that this cooperation will be fragile by nature.[78] Based on these presumptions, NATO (Risse-Kappen's case study) has many of the characteristics of a security community because of the shared values among its member-states. It is therefore because of these shared values and norms of procedure that Risse-Kappen contends that the smaller member-states are able to influence the larger ones. The reasoning behind this assumption is that the interests and identity of a large country are altered. Those of the United States become, because of this sense of shared values, intertwined with those of its European allies, and visa versa. As the author states, differences between interest-driven and value-guided behaviour lessen, while the scope for cooperation grows.[79]

In the concluding section of the work, Risse-Kappen reiterates that statements and actions by one or more of the allies illustrate the identification of these member-states which each other. He suggests that this sentiment is due to institutional processes of decision making that stem from a set of shared values and norms. Only in a minority of instances was a lack of cooperation present, and by definition the absence of a shared sense of community. To this end, the findings add to an already growing literature that analyses this issue in the examination of world politics, and therefore more, rather than less, research into the role and impact of ideas in international relations should be conducted.[80]

Similarly, Keohane and Goldstein in their co-authored *Ideas and foreign policy* assert that their book is 'about how ideas, which we define as beliefs held by individuals, help to explain political outcomes'.[81] They believe that ideas do influence policy. Therefore their approach is about moving from a static rationalist analysis of politics to a transformative one. They claim that ideas are endogenous to the process of policy making, rather than assumed, ignored, taken for granted or considered to be external to this process, as in rationalist approaches. And it is precisely because of the dominance of these rationalist approaches that the co-authors contend that there is a need to bring ideas back into the discourse of international relations.

There are three types of ideas that the co-authors speak of: world views, principled beliefs and causal beliefs. The first includes religious persuasion, ideologies such as Communism and/or concepts such as sovereignty. The second type consists of normative beliefs such as 'slavery is wrong' or that all have a 'right to free speech'. Causal beliefs, on the other hand, are those that derive authority from a consensus among recognized elites, scientists, village elders or like groupings.[82] In turn, all three may affect policy in different ways. These include ideas acting as road maps, affecting strategies where there is no equilibrium, or by becoming embedded in institutions.[83] The authors assert that regardless of which of these types of impact are present, ideas matter. How, to what extent, and in what way, shape or form are other important questions associated with this type of non-rationalist work, but are secondary the initial stance. That ideas count and play a role in the creation of policy are not under discussion.

When ideas are not ideas

Thomas Risse-Kappen spends a great deal of time attempting to convince the reader that when he speaks about shared values he is speaking about ideas. What appears so unconvincing about this approach is how he defines a liberal theory of international relations and the role, if any, of ideas within this theorization. In the introductory chapter of his book Risse-Kappen clarifies what he means by a *liberal* theory of international relations. This includes: a belief in agents as defined as individuals rather than states acting in a social context; the analysis of interests and preferences as products of the social structure of the international system as well as domestic political concerns; and that international institutions form these social structures that then constrain or encourage government actions.[84] The first two points sound similar to a Gramscian analysis of international relations through the language of 'social structures' and an interest in agency that is broader than that of statism. However, it is the third and final point that breaks this cord between the two approaches. For Gramsci, ideas shape institutional preferences as well as how material capabilities will be used, which materials will be built and why. In turn, the last two factors dialectically impact upon these initial ideas. The terrain of civil society, in which these factors are present, is constantly being used as a battleground of dominance and resistance between them with respect to which set of forces are more determinant than the others, which in turn creates an environment for another movement of resistance. At no one time are all three of these sets of forces equal in their importance, but one is never constantly more important than the others. This does not appear to be the case with the liberal theory described by Risse-Kappen. Institutions and their processes (norms, rules and patterns of behaviour), rather than ideas and/or material capabilities, appear to be *the* most important set of forces of the three at all times, rather than only at some times. In such a scenario, a dialectic cannot be sustained, even if present, and neither can a constant state of dominance and resistance be at the heart of the terrain of civil society. Again, there is talk of ideas, but it appears not to be the language of Gramsci that is being spoken.

This criticism is also true of the approach of Keohane and Goldstein and the works that Risse-Kappen cites in his conclusion as those that also report research into the role of ideas in international relations, such as John Ruggie. They are institution oriented and thus their premise is based in this language of ideas, but rooted concretely in norms and rules, which are not the same as the social context and terrain that Gramsci, as well as Cox, speak of. For example, in an edited volume on principles, norms, rules and decision-making procedures, principles are described as 'beliefs of fact, causation, and rectitude' whereas norms are considered to be standards of behaviour defined in terms of rights and duties.[85] By and large, these appear not to be the same definitions as those of Cox. Further, Keohane and Goldstein speak of *individual* rather than *collective* ideas. Added to this is the caveat that these individual ideas appear to become relevant only when they meet a number of conditions. These include when ideas serve as road maps, when the situation is at equilibrium and therefore the ideas would serve some purpose and have some impact, or when they become embedded in institutions.[86] Therefore, for the co-authors to make the point that they believe ideas matter must be taken with a degree of qualification, for they assert that ideas count only given certain conditions and the proper environment, rather than without prejudice. For Gramsci and Cox, ideas count both individually and collectively, and do so without conditionality. As Rise-Kappen ties ideas to institutions, so too do Keohane and Goldstein, whereas for Gramsci and Cox ideas – collective images of world order – stand alongside other forces such as institutional processes and material capabilities, but are never referred to as being subordinate to either, or both.

Ruggie's work, in spite of its talk of collective existence, is one example of theories that lean backwards to institutionalism as the basis upon which they premise their arguments. Ruggie does this, and more, to lessen the critical theoretical orientation of his argument and to unbundle the problematic notion of territoriality.[87] Ruggie speaks of the potential creation of a new collective existence based upon the issues surrounding global ecology.

There is the possibility to create a new and very different social episteme, taking into consideration forces such as spatial, metaphysical and doctrinal constructs.[88] However, while speaking a language resembling that of Gramsci and Cox in both of his articles on forms of institutions and transformative processes, Ruggie falls short of a critical theoretical position on two accounts. Ruggie backs to two positions that are both unreflexive, lacking in transformative potential and rationalist in their premises. In one instance he states that the constructivist work of Alexander Wendt should be perceived as 'one recent attempt to formulate an ontology of international relations that is predicated on the need to endogenize the origins of structures and preferences, if transformation is to be understood'.[89] Or, instead of appealing to the scientific realism of Wendt, Ruggie suggests that another option is to examine the utility of the concept of 'multiperspective institutional forms', which may offer a 'lens through which to view other possible instances of international transformation today'.[90] One example given by the author as an area of potential research that may illustrate this capacity is the concept of international custodianship. He stresses this institutional bias with reference to European security. The claim is that all the suggestions before us with respect to achieving security in Europe are multilateral and institutional in form, and therefore this multiperspective institutional concept may have much to tell us about transformation in international relations.[91] However, a return to institutionalism is not the same as the 'fit' spoken of by Gramsci and Cox, where a dialectic between the three forces exists, rather than an eternal dominance by one. One can, therefore, notice a streak of rationalism in the work of Ruggie and others like him. Thus it is useful as a starting rather than an endpoint in this discussion of the transitional politics of the EBRD, and also helps to explain why a move to a postmodern critical theoretical perspective is not only useful, but necessary.

However, because of the problems associated with the post-modern project to alluded above, but still cognizant of the need for a critical theoretical solution, the turn to a Gramscian-inspired approach is even more understandable in this context.

Finally, and what also separates the Keohane/Goldstein approach from that of Gramsci/Cox, is the reflexive and critical nature of the latter in comparison with the still more than slightly rationalist position of the former. First, Keohane and Goldstein make the point that the relationship between ideas and shifts in material power is complex, and do not all run in one direction.[92] Therefore the relationship between these two factors may be dialectical, but may be not. The authors are unsure and thus wary of making any claims. There is no doubt in a Gramscian analysis of this. All three – ideas, institutions and material capabilities – operate within a complex and overlapping dialectical relationship that is multidirectional. This position grows directly out of the Marxist nature of Gramsci's thoerization and points to a significant breach between these approaches. Second, because of this dialectic, a Gramscian paradigm is by nature critical theoretical rather than problem solving in its appearance. In order to be so, it purposely operates from outside the system it seeks to explain. In comparison, Keohane and Goldstein are open about their adherence to a number of rationalist arguments, including their interest in empiricism, public policy problem solving and self-interested behaviour.[93] The admission by Peter Haas that the 'epistemic community' research[94] is grounded in knowledge-based information as regards what are defined as ideas is indicative not only of this rationalist approach, but also of the theoretical gaps that cannot be bridged between Keohane and Goldstein, and Gramsci and Cox.

Wendt's work is of a different nature. Here is a constructivist who speaks about intersubjective meanings in the formation of identities and interests, and defines them in a very Gramscian manner. As stated above, these meanings can be conceived as being shared understandings, expectations and social knowledge embedded in international institutions and threat complexes. Even if one factors out those that pertain to international institutions, left are those that sound Gramsci-like in orientation. Moreover, the entirety of Wendt's work also sounds as such, making more problematic the question of how one distinguishes between one who speaks like a Gramscian, and one who is Gramscian in engagement and application. In short, what divides rather than brings together the approaches of this work on the one hand and that of Wendt on the other?

In an article summarizing Alexander Wendt's work, Erik Ringmar notes two distinct periods in his academic career. The first is characterized by his status as a structuralist with a realist orientation – in other words, a scientific realist. The second, and more relevant, period of his career has been marked by an interest in constructivism as a means of moving beyond this earlier rationalist position. Ringmar posits that this shift might have taken place because of a lack of faith in the ability of a realist oriented project to bridge the so-called agent–structure gap that Wendt has written much about because of its lack of trans-formative abilities. In response, there was a move on Wendt's part to a language of social interaction rather than structure.[95] One of the more recent recitations of this turn has already been explored above, so here will be highlighted Wendt's inability to move substantially to this language of intersubjective meanings without the constraints and baggage of his earlier scientific realist leanings.

Ringmar makes the point that while Waltz is used as the foil in order for this turn to be made, it is a turn made unsuccessfully. Evidence of this failing is the academic's continued return to rationalism. At first, he argues from an idealist stance, in that a materialist perspective does not take knowledge into account.

Therefore balances of *power* are less important than balances of *threat* perception.[96] This knowledge is tied up in a structure that gives it a greater and collective meaning. By being processed in this manner, knowledge can impact upon international relations by giving the latter meaning through representation. A consequence of this approach is that Wendt is able to understand Waltz's anarchy in terms of the distribution of material power and the representational meanings of this power. Anarchy, in short, depends on one's (i.e. a state's) understanding of this situation rather than the situation itself.[97] The implications of this position are twofold. First, rather than having only agents and structures, there is now a third force – social practice – operating between the two. The second is that identities can now be formed from a basis of social practice – representation and inter-subjectivity – as well as materialism, rather than only the latter. A broader conception of 'what is' is the product of this constructivist thought balanced on top of a rationalist approach.

It is, however, the attempt by Wendt to remain a scientific realist while simultaneously adopting a constructivist approach that finally illustrates the inherent tension in this position. It is also this tension that indicates the theoretical differences between Wendt's constructivism and the Gramscian paradigm of Cox. To be a constructivist, one cannot rely on the representations of material facts, because material facts are not facts per se. They are, like everything else, created by people rather than actually existing in their own right. One believes in either material facts or representation, but not both. For Gramsci and Cox this tension does not exist for there is never the intention of being either a scientific realist nor a constructivist where only representation lives. For the latter, it is a fit between representations (ideas) and materialism, along with institutional processes, that makes the world go round. And it is a world that is dialectical, whereas for Wendt it is a world based upon a unidirectional relationship between materialism and representation, where the former informs the latter without any apparent reciprocation. Finally, and as Ringmar asserts, even without the baggage of scientific realism, the constructivism of Wendt has problems in that it is the social practice of states that informs these representations. For Ringmar this entails a number of difficulties. In the case of whether or not Wendt is Gramsci-like, a set of other problems arise from this position. By maintaining a scientific realist approach that is biased towards structures and states, ideas, intersubjective meanings and identities lose their importance as forces in and of themselves. They become objects rather than subjects of inquiry, and therefore the dialectic that Gramsci requires between ideas, capabilities and institutions is rejected in favour of a unidirectional, top-down relationship between what counts and what is counted. Wendt returns, rather, to the traditionalist billiard ball (given A, B will occur…) approach to international relations. The implication of this is that Wendt's constructivism is rather static and structural instead of innovative, theoretically challenging and transformative. Exclusion is opted for instead of inclusiveness of those forces – identities and intersubjective meanings – that he initially spoke of as being critical to understanding the world in which states and other actors operate.

Summary

In all three instances – Risse-Kappen, Keohane and Goldstein, and Wendt – the language employed sounds like that of Gramsci and Cox. However, it is evident upon further research that though the language may sound similar, the methodology and ontology are quite different. All three purport to overcome the constraints of rationalist arguments, but none succeeds. Through their failings, the ideas they speak of become subject to empiricist and other non-dialectical concerns that illustrate this gap between their approaches and that of Gramsci and Cox. Therefore while the Gramscian Marxism applied in this work may not be identical to either that which can be found in *The prison notebooks* or in *Production, power and world order*, this author has attempted, by way of a similar use of ideas, to stay true to the intentions of Gramsci and Cox while adapting their work for the sake of applicability in a matter pertaining to the 'hard case' of strategic studies rather than the 'softer' one of political economy.

Having said this, the concerns raised by the Burnham and Kenny and Germain articles are important to note and investigate. It is crucial if one is to invoke a certain theorization and tradition that one does not get it wrong and in doing so appear to sound more like those writing from another school of thought. This paradigmatic error would serve only to damage one's project. But by flagging up these points of concern, and addressing these issues in a forthright manner, they can be an aid if gaps between these secondary approaches and the one intended to be used become apparent, as has been the case above through an exploration of pluralist and constructivist accounts of international relations. But where does this leave one? Given the lack of autonomy accorded 'ideas' in both the constructivism of Wendt and the institutionalism of Keohane, Goldstein and Risse-Kappen, one is forced to turn to even more alternative approaches to international relations for a perspective that not only talks about the importance of ideas alongside other factors, but acts upon that importance throughout its logic.

Having gone through this process only slightly scathed, it is not enough to not present an alternative scenario of the above case study from the vantage of point of one's desired paradigm. How should this be done without reducing one's alternative to the foundationalism of realism or losing the essence of the approach along the way? This will be the task of the next section.

For Mearsheimer is correct. It is not enough to assert and highlight 'contradictions', as has already been accomplished in the preceding chapter. What is required is an explication of an alternative scenario to, in this instance, economic transition that embraces the constituent elements of Cox's Gramscian approach without the rationalist and structuralist qualities of Oakeshott, Waltz and open Marxism.

The application of the Coxian paradigm

The early years

The EBRD underwent numerous changes after its first two years. Many of these changes improved how, when, at what level and in what manner policies are made, approved and implemented. Senior management and the Board of Directors agreed on a general strategy for the institution that included a number of basic lending guidelines, these being solid banking and conditionality criteria and transitional impact guarantees. These outcomes of the strategic review also addressed the role of the institution relative to similar non-governmental organizations such as the World Bank and IMF. Transitional reports are now produced annually to serve as reminders of not only the progress of recipient member-states but also these strategic conditions. As stated above, all these changes and the reasoning behind them can be accounted for by one, two or even parts of all three paradigms examined earlier in this chapter. What could not be done by any of the three is a comprehensive elaboration of these events. It is the intention of this author to illustrate here that it is the Coxian paradigm, when applied to the above changes, that can deliver this comprehensive understanding.

In order for this comprehensiveness to take hold, what must come to the fore at the outset is the position that ideas not only played a significant role in the shaping and administration of the EBRD in its first two years, but also during the next three years. The *Transition reports*, alongside the contradictions found within the three new guidelines, indicated that the debate over 'ideas' and what Central and Eastern Europe should resemble in the future has not subsided. The fact that the reports are unable to issue a clear and unequivocal definition of a 'market' is representative of this continuing battle of ideas between, roughly, the Anglo-Saxon and continental European member-states. That US and French officials continued to disagree over the same issues two and three years on is another illustration of this same lack of agreement with respect to the ideas that should shape the direction of the EBRD. These and other points merely serve to remind one that what is required to understand these debates and disagreements is a paradigm that is wary of scientific and objective measurements and is instead inclusive of factors that are ideas based. This inclusiveness is required because what occurred at the EBRD was a battle for control of the manner in which decisions were made and taken, for the hegemonic control of the organization.

The leadership of the United States is aware that on a given issue, per se, continental European countries, along with like-minded member-states, are able to block its interests. This leadership is also aware that because the United States controls only 10 per cent of the voting rights it must change through other means and avenues the way in which the Bank makes decisions. In Gramscian terms, the ability to attain hegemony within the EBRD through material means (voting) was not possible, thus a different and more indirect approach had to be taken. The leadership of the United States had to change the way in which countries thought about the institution prior to the attainment of an ideas-based type of hegemony.

To do so, the leadership of the United States had to mitigate the usefulness of the institution whenever possible. To detract attention from the reality of the situation in the early 1990s, the United States managed to cast doubt upon the senior management of the institution. The firing of Attali precipitated a strategic review of the institution as well as the selection of a new President who would be more acceptable to the United States. The strategic review was the opportunity for the United States, like the initial negotiations leading up to the establishment of the Bank, to put into place a series of guidelines and criteria that would bias its ideas-based material interests. The fact that the notion of 'sound banking' is the first of the three new principles is, as mentioned above, not coincidental. That 'transition impact' is now conceived of in a private sector rather than traditional 'development' manner is also not surprising. The view that the EBRD should not receive an increase in its capitalization, and therefore must depend on profits from initial loans, thus forcing the institution to be even more focused on these notions of 'sound banking' and a private sector oriented 'transition impact', is also not coincidental. That the EBRD must work with the more established IMF and World Bank, and be viewed by many as the lesser of the three and become marginalized over time, is also part of a much larger whole. And the list of measures proposed and put into practice by the EBRD at the behest of the United States is endless, but need not be mentioned. Simply put, if the EBRD begins to be perceived by third parties and member-states as 'one of the many' rather than 'the' institution assisting Central and Eastern Europe, there will not be the desire of previously supportive countries to come to its rescue. In turn, the United States and like-minded countries will continue to press for ideas-based changes that fit with their interests.

The above illustrates an interesting fit between institutional change and institutionalism, material capabilities and interests and the presence and use of ideas in the shaping of policy. The United States has certain ideas concerning the way in which an economic system for a CEEC should be developed over time. One vehicle through which these ideas can be acted upon is the EBRD. But do to so the Bank required changes in its senior management, decision-making structures and goals and objectives so that they were more conducive to Anglo-Saxon thinking. By fixing a ceiling on the capitalization of the EBRD by rejecting any increase its capitalization through member-state contributions, the United States, in part, has driven the Bank to become more profit oriented. This orientation, coupled with changes to its objectives and the introduction of new guidelines for lending and a new decision-making structure, is now more in line with US ideas concerning the development of market economies in Central and Eastern Europe. The hiring of a more US-friendly President with 'banking' experience and raising of the profile of an experienced merchant banker and the merchant banking sector within the EBRD are but additives to this overall project of the United States.

Thus ideas, institutions and material capabilities were linked to produce a strategy whereby an Anglo-Saxon perspective of transition would become, over time, 'hegemonic' within the decision-making structures of the EBRD. This attempt is apparent given that some of the continental European countries are concerned enough that old issues that engendered disagreements, such as the privatization/restructuring debate, are now resurfacing. This is true of similar issues and, as noted earlier, can be seen by the way in which the *Transition reports* showed signs of a hesitancy to take a stance with respect to the definition of certain concepts and terms, such as what constitutes a 'market'. Observers and people involved in the day-to-day workings of the EBRD are witnessing a subtle, yet concerted and powerful, attempt on the part of the United States and like-minded countries to 'overthrow' the ideas-based hegemony of continental Europe and replace it with an Anglo-Saxon variant. Unlike a Weberian notion of hegemony, this one is based on a crucial interplay of various factors, each underpinning and strengthening the others in the production of a powerful argument against the 'status quo' position, and in favour of a new perspective.

Institution building

The previous section illustrates that, when attempting to understand the post-1992 cooperation between the European countries and the United States, a more 'critical', comprehensive and 'ideas-based' approach to understanding cooperation is warranted. However, this has come mainly in the area of cooperation between the Western allies in the post-1992 phase of the EBRD. Can and should this more 'critical' approach to international relations also be utilized for the attainment of a better understanding of the initial phase of the EBRD (considered in the next session) and our more general conception of institution building?

Steven Weber makes two interesting comments with respect to institution building and the EBRD that appear to be relevant to this discussion. He asserts that 'ideas played an important role in the EBRD's birthright'.[98] Weber also states that 'although the states that created EBRD disagreed (and continue to disagree) over the specifics of implementation, they gained remarkably quickly a consensus on the legitimacy and centrality of the institution's distinctive identity and goals'.[99] What is interesting to note with respect to both these comments is the use of the past tense, in that once the negotiations establishing the EBRD were concluded, ideas ceased to be fundamentally important in the operation of the organization. Also, because ideas stopped being important once negotiations ceased, disagreements between the dominant member-states could not be ideas based, but centred, rather, on the of the day-to-day administration of the EBRD.

The brief analysis above of the lending policies of the EBRD highlights a story different from that told by Weber. Although demonstrating that there are numerous variables in understanding why and how an institution such as the EBRD is established, most significant is the continued importance of 'ideas', even after the EBRD became fully operational. This was most likely so because issues that were fundamentally ideas based were subject to compromise and 'fudging' on the part of all the dominant member-states. I use the word 'fudging' because, while compromise is always a feature of a negotiating session, what occurred with respect to the EBRD was that the dominant states publicly agreed to a series of compromises but privately desired to 'renegotiate' these compromises through slight, but ongoing, changes in the day-to-day lending policies of the institution. This 'fudging' may have been altruistically motivated, in that the Western allies may have decided that the CEECs could not wait for assistance, thus making compromise of fundamental concerns the less than optimal, but necessary, outcome of the negotiations. Nonetheless, this fudging of the issues had and continues to have serious implications for the operations of the EBRD, as well as its clients in need. One example of this 'fudging' was the decision to codify a lending policy that would prioritize the private sector over the public. This decision was not disliked by most of the negotiators for the EC member-states, but they would have preferred a more flexible arrangement, an arrangement that they hoped would develop over time anyway given the fluid economic conditions of the CEECs. Also, the leadership of the United States would have rather seen the EBRD develop a lending policy that was almost totally private sector oriented. Consequently, it would appear that ideas played a role not only during negotiations, but afterwards as well.

The question then is if one cannot fully explain the activities of the EBRD through an 'environment-based' model like that used by Weber, what model of institution building should one proceed with? Giulio Gallarotti concludes that one can conceive of multiple reasons for the failure of an organization. These include problems arising from the management of complex and tightly coupled systems; adverse substitution; dispute intensification; and moral hazard.[100]

While during the life of an organization all of these concerns will appear individually or in differing combinations, the one that is most relevant to this analysis of the EBRD is dispute intensification. This is, as Gallarotti points out, opposite from what most scholars tend to see as the function of formal and informal organizations and regimes, which is the reduction of disputes through the creation of channels of communication, the increase in the amount of perfect knowledge and the ability of actors to predict the behaviour of allies or enemies.

Gallarotti posits that Inis Claude is correct when he claims that international organizations often function as arenas for the conduct of international warfare. Claude's example of this instance is the United Nations, and in particular the (historical) relationship between the Western powers and Soviet Union in the Security Council. Instead of perceiving the Security Council as a forum in which differences could be solved, the organization became the forum through which opposing states widened conflict through insult, inflammatory speeches and terminology, and the use of the veto. Instead of a means by which the Cold War could be laid to rest, the United Nations became another arena of East–West, as well as north–south, competition.

The EBRD can be located within this context of dispute intensification for a number of reasons. First, it is because the states within the EBRD were, and continue to be, allies that the disagreements concerning economic systems and operational policies are notable. Second, these allies are such not only because of shared security concerns, but also because they are perceived

to hold similar perspectives with respect to economic development, the need for market-based economic systems and the role
of the state in the economy. Third, it is because of the institutional
environment that Western states operate in, from the IMF and
GATT to NATO, that one might expect a greater amount of
understanding and cooperation than that which occurred. Given
that all of these states agreed, in the wake of World War Two, to
the creation of the liberal international economic order and its
representative institutions, one might be led to believe that
arguments concerning the role of the state, the need for market-
based economies and the correct manner in which a formerly
centrally planned country should transform itself would have
been settled forty years ago. Also, it is because these states are
dependent on each other for their individual and collective
security, in the broadest sense, that one would again presume that
the disagreements that occurred should not have.

Such disagreements would appear to go against conventional
wisdom. The question then is why, and what can we learn about
the creation and maintenance of institutions from this episode? In
the United States there is a 'tradition of anti-government bias,
and … the deep-seated U.S. preference for keeping the public and
private sectors as separate as possible'.[101] On the other hand,
Germany 'takes a … quintessential community approach'.[102]
Given that there is not only a degree of similarity between these
allies but also differences in their approaches to economic
development and systems, the codification of these beliefs within
some type of formal document may serve only to exacerbate
these differences and push aside the similarities. This may be so
because negotiations, writ large, tend to focus on the former
rather than the latter only because there is no need to state
explicitly what is already known and common. The desire of the
United States to codify its prioritization of the private sector over
the public was an act that enhanced disagreement rather than

dampened it. The disagreements between the allies with respect to this, and related issues, became tense because the member-states of the EC desired to illustrate the 'Europeaness' of the EBRD to the United States and could do so only by quietly demonstrating their initial and continued displeasure with the stance of the United States.

It seems that the Americans took any opportunity to oppose the 'Europeaness' of the EBRD.[103] Given that there was a lack of disagreement with respect to how the G-24 was assisting CEECs, the creation of an institution to do what was already being done may appear to have been a superfluous initiative, not driven by the need for greater efficiency and effectiveness but by the need to be seen to be 'doing something' for Central and Eastern Europe. In contrast, the ad hoc arrangements that had charac-terized the Western response to the transition of CEECs to market-based economic systems were not fraught with as many significant disagreements as was the EBRD. Again, this may have been because of the lack of a need for a set of codified objectives, goals and priorities on the part of the Western allies. The lack of divergence prior to the establishment of the EBRD may imply that the creation of an institution is not the optimum decision reached by a group of actors, regardless of the reasons that institution is desired. To this end, Gallarotti suggests that a 'better approach' to institution building is of a limited type and kind.[104]

Gallarotti speaks of international organizations failing when certain incorrect presumptions concerning their utility is made on the part of their creators. First, organizations often fail because their vagueness encourages rule breaking and free riding. Second, they fail when the conditions that require management are overestimated, such as the predatory nature of nation-states in an anarchic environment. Third, actors tend to look for disorder even if there is none. This often results in the creation of organizations for the sake of being seen to 'do something'. However, Keohane and Nye point out that 'issues lacking conflicts of interest may need very little institutional form'.[105] Last, organizations are often formed in order to reduce costs deriving from asymmetrical information, deception, irresponsibility, uncertainty, risk and unstable expectations. But if these costs are not present or are slight, then a regime may be more appropriate than a formal organization.

While a number of the reasons why limited or informal organizations may work better than more formal institutions are irrelevant to the problems of the EBRD, some are, and present us with other queries. Instead of being too vague, the problem with the EBRD might have been its lack of vagueness, and the absence of costs such as risk, irresponsibility and the presence of imperfect or asymmetrical information as key determinants in the creation of the EBRD. While there may have been 'disorder', it might not have been of the type that Gallarotti presumes, which is more politico-military in character than economic. Consequently, the one factor cited above that makes sense with respect to the EBRD is the being seen to 'do something' hypothesis. But this begs the question of why an organization is created in the first place. In the case of the EBRD, Weber does make the point that, rather than attempting to explain the creation of the Bank in terms of economic efficiency and measurable outputs, one is on more solid ground by speaking of the 'appropriateness of the form' of the institution in question, where means and ends are divorced from each other, and 'social fitness' is more important.[106] If this was true in the case of the EBRD, then it might be true to say that a more informal organizational structure, if needed at all, might have been more appropriate. Of course, it is of interest to note that the leadership of the United States was not in favour of the creation of a new institution from the outset, and became engaged only when it discovered that the EBRD would be created with or without their presence. Instead, the expansion of the roles of the IMF and/or World Bank, alongside the programmes of the G-24, were the proposals forwarded by the United States. However, because these proposals were seen as a means of continuing US dominance at the expense of the member-states of the EC, all of them were rejected by the latter. Had these initiatives been perceived as being more mutually beneficial than they were, a more informal arrangement may have been accepted by the EC. Instead, the EBRD was born of the desire of the EC to be seen assuming responsibility for events taking place in Europe, to be seen to be 'doing something concrete' for Central and Eastern Europe. In this respect, the EBRD was desirable for its own sake, much to the chagrin of Keohane and Nye, who have come to conclusion that this is often not the case.

At this juncture it may be useful to summarize a number of key points. A first would be that, in comparison with Weber's analysis, ideas will continue to 'count' in the day-to-day administration of the EBRD's operation and policies. The second would be that it may be incorrect to assume that the member-states have congruent ideas with respect to economic development, market-based systems and the role of the state in an economy simply because they are long-standing allies in the areas of security and economic relations. Third, it may be because of the presence of conflicting ideas that a formal institution with a definitive set of guidelines and rules such as the EBRD was exactly not what should have been arranged in order to assist the transitional economies of CEECs. The need to create a formal document most likely assisted not only in dramatizing Western differences, but also in delaying assistance to the CEECs. Rather, the creation of a regime that would have been something more than the ad hoc agreements that existed prior to the EBRD but something less than the EBRD would have been the optimum decision on the part of the Western allies.

This analysis, with respect to theories of international relations and an understanding of international organizations, begs a final question: if power-based or utilitarian-based theories cannot account for the role of 'ideas', and neither can the analysis of Weber, where does one turn to theoretically? One answer might be towards the 'epistemic communities' paradigm of Peter Haas that has already been examined in this book, albeit in a different context. As noted previously, Haas' notion of these communities are such that one might be able to conclude that 'ideas' flow upwards in an organization from the presence of like-minded knowledge-based experts at the lower and middle levels of management. However, as was also noted previously, these experts are facts based. The difficulty here is that even Weber speaks of 'ideas' in a more intersubjective manner than Haas. Second, and with specific reference to the EBRD, knowledge-based experts failed to sway the leadership of the United States with respect to certain key policy decisions even when there was consensus among these experts. Thus the epistemic community argument falls short on two counts – that it is not 'ideas based' in accordance with how Weber defines 'ideas' in his article, and that these communities were not influential in the decision-making process of the EBRD.

It is, at the end of the day, because of this failure on the part of Haas and others dealing with institutions and institution building that one is again drawn to a realization that what is warranted is a more 'critical' and alternative theorization of politics. To this end, I return to the Gramscian-styled paradigm of Robert Cox and ask whether it is able to assist in explaining the institutional aspects of the EBRD in the same manner as it has been able to with respect to cooperation within the context of the Bank after 1992. As noted previously, Cox speaks of ideas in two contexts. The first is that ideas fit into two broad categories, the first being intersubjective meanings and shared notions of social relations and the second that are collective images of social order that are held by different groups of people, which in turn may, or may not, produce a clash of 'ideas' which are then played out through institutions or a variety of actions at the level of the international system.[107] The second is that these ideas do not operate in a political vacuum. They, along with institutional processes and material capabilities, produce a 'fit' that allows one to understand politics, and in particular interstate relations, in a more comprehensive manner than traditional theories of politics. The question then is how is this Coxian 'fit' relevant to the pre-1992 phase of the EBRD?

The EBRD

Most of the major disagreements between the member-states of the EC and the United States concerned the implementation of a certain type of market-based economic system, the use of a certain model of economic development for transitional states and whether or not the state, in general, should have a role in the economic affairs of a population. Even other issues such as the status of the EIB and the Soviet Union were, to a certain extent, minor manifestations of this larger quarrel. Clashes between the allies over lending policies, 'soft loans' and restructuring and/or privatization were the more obvious indicators of these economic policy-related disagreements. However, what is common between all these disputes is that they were disputes concerning 'ideas' and how ideas would affect the policies of an institution, and in turn how this institution would be able to utilize its material capabilities. Thus one might be able to place these disagreements within the context of Cox's theorization, given that these arguments did concern the material capabilities of the donor and recipient countries, an institutional framework and 'ideas' that were intersubjective and concerned the thoughts of particular groups with respect to the creation of social, political and economic order. Thus instead of utilizing traditional theories of international relations such as neorealism and neoliberalism, or those specific to organizational theory, one might be better off with respect to the understanding of ideas-based institutional disagreements among allies through the utilization of Robert Cox's Gramscian Marxist theorization of international politics.

Lessons for the Bretton Woods institutions?

Given that there needs to be a better appreciation of the 'fit' between institutional processes (policies), material capabilities (capital and member-states' voting rights) and ideas with respect to the establishment and maintenance of an institution, are there lessons than can be learned in the building of post-Cold War institutions in Europe from the experience of the allies within the context of the EBRD? Given that the Bretton Woods institutions (IMF, World Bank and GATT, or at least the World Trade Organization, which replaced it in 1995) are now over fifty years old and facing a period of reassessment, are there any lessons that can learnt from the EBRD experience and adapted to these other institutions?[108]

The case of the EBRD reveals significant allied differences with respect to economic development, the role of the state in economic issues and other related matters. It would therefore appear obvious that these ideas-based differences will also be present within other political economic organizations, especially when a period of reassessment occurs. The restructuring of political economic institutions will need to reflect interest-based differences as well as changes in the overall global political economic environment, such as the resurgent strength of the EU and its relative position to the United States in world economic affairs, as well as other rising powers, most notably in Asia.

However, the battleground during this period of reassessment will also be shaped by the prioritization of differing economic models of development held by Western Europe and the United States. One can imagine that what has occurred within the confines of the EBRD will be replicated in the World Trade Organization over issues such as the subsidization of industrial development and the IMF and World Bank with respect to the role of the private sector in the development of non-Western economies.

But should this inclusion of ideas-based factors in the determination of Western relations come as such a surprise? The relationship between institutional arrangements and policy orientation was first mooted in an article by John Ruggie that dealt with the issue of 'embedded liberalism' and the formation of the post-World War Two liberal international economic order.[109] After analysing the form and content of Bretton Woods institutions, Ruggie contended that all these institutions and regimes had some degree of 'social purpose' embedded in them by their founders – the Unites States and the United Kingdom. To Ruggie, this 'social purpose' content reflected the ideas and beliefs of these countries, ideas and beliefs that allowed these institutions and regimes to maintain themselves even after the end of overt US political economic hegemony in the late 1960s and early 1970s. Thus, rather than the presence of political economic chaos from the mid-1970s onward, because of the relative loss of hegemony and power on the part of the United States, there has been an absence of overall disagreement with the fundamental goals of the Bretton Woods era, these being open markets, market-based economic systems and trade liberalism. Simply put, for Ruggie, ideas matter in the formulation of informal and formal institutions, and if not accounted for and understood as autonomous and important factors, the institutions that are constructed may falter in this lack of understanding.

It is exactly this confluence of form (organizational structure) and content (social purpose) that is absent from Weber's analysis of the EBRD and other traditional attempts to comprehend the formulation of institutions – formal and informal alike. However, it is this confluence that is understood and developed in the Coxian paradigm and is, in the opinion of this author, critical to understanding the problems and allied disagreements that plagued the EBRD from the outset of its establishment. Thus as was the case with our understanding of the post-1992 phase of the EBRD, the application of a Coxian analysis to the initial years of the Bank can prove fruitful in the development of a richer understanding of how the institution was established, why it was plagued with disagreements in its first year and most importantly why similar types of issues reappeared after only one year of operation.

It is also this confluence of form and content that is critical to our understanding of the disputes that have, are and will occur in the future within the context of existing allies-dominated political economic institutions. The disputes between the United States and its allies within the context of the World Bank, IFC and other multilateral development banks that have been illustrated in chapter 3 mirror those present in the EBRD for two reasons. The first is that the issues were similar in that they were about lending policies and, in general, the role of the state in the economic life of a country. The second similarity is that these disputes were also about 'ideas', and the clash of them between the major member-states of these institutions. More importantly, and again like the EBRD, the institutional processes of these institutions (lending policies), how these institutions would utilize their material capabilities (capital) and how the dominant member-states would use their material capabilities (voting rights) were coupled with 'ideas' concerning economic management and development to produce a major disagreement between member-states. Given that many of these institutions are facing a period of reassessment in the wake of their fiftieth anniversaries, one might posit that disputes concerning lending policies, institutional processes and capabilities will come to the fore. In our search for an explanation of these debates, we must not lose sight of the crucial role that 'ideas' have and will play in their settlement. If the politicians, diplomats and academics conducting these reassessments focus solely on form, they will not address the underlying and fundamental issues associated with these institutions. This ignoring of the role played by 'ideas' would therefore be, as we have witnessed with the EBRD, to the detriment of the longevity and utility of these institutions.

Institution building for the future

The same warnings with respect to form and content should be put to those who are interested in establishing institutions similar to the EBRD. Simply put, member-states can agree on the institutional processes and material capabilities of a new institution, but if the form or ideas of this institution are not agreed to, then its usefulness will be placed in jeopardy. One possible example may be the proposed development bank for the Middle East. In the wake of peace treaties between Israel and Jordan and Israel and the Palestine Liberation Organization, which led to the establishment of the Palestinian National Authority, many politicians have spoken about the rise of the 'new Middle East'.[110] For these politicians there is the expectation that trade will flourish between these countries, tapping the economic potential of the entire region. President Clinton spoke of the creation of a development bank, funded by Western Europe, Japan and the United States, that would assist in unlocking this potential and making the 'new Middle East' a reality. The goals of the proposed institution are to assist in the building of transborder infrastructure projects; the invigoration of the private sector and stimulation of private capital flows; the establishment of a regional policy dialogue; and overall reform, liberalization and integration of the regional economy.[111] Like the EBRD, this development bank would consist of over forty members, with the EU, Japan and the United States being the primary donors of the expected \$5 billion capital base. It is also posited that the bank should be self-financing, by lending at market rates. However, it has been mooted that 'soft loans' to entities such as the Palestinian National Authority may be necessary. Finally, and as was the case with the EBRD when it was proposed by Mitterrand, there is some hesitancy about the creation of such an institution. The US Treasury Department, along with the member-states of the EU, Saudi Arabia and some of the Gulf states, have expressed reservations about the need for such a bank. Officials claim that this development bank would overlap not only with the World Bank and IMF, but also existing regional structures. In response, the US Secretary of State, Warren Christopher, stated that the bank would 'complement and not duplicate the work of the World Bank and IMF' and would serve to assist and underpin the ongoing peace process by linking the economies of the various states through, primarily, transborder projects.[112]

This proposed Middle East development bank sounds very much like the EBRD. In fact, *The Guardian* stated that the proposals for this bank, in October 1994 in Casablanca, were modelled on the EBRD. Thus it is not surprising that there are many similarities in its goals and those of the EBRD, especially regarding the possibility of 'soft loans'. However, the lessons of the EBRD need to be headed. It was not enough for these allies to agree to an institution, invest in it a sizeable amount of capital and produce a well meaning charter of principles, and then assume that the institution in question will be able to operate effectively. What these allies forgot, or failed to take into consideration, or understood but decided to ignore, was that an institution devoid of an agreed set of ideas (content) will be unable to put into practice its processes and capabilities. Given the long-standing differences between the countries of the Middle East, coupled with the ideas-based differences of the Western allies as seen by the disputes in the EBRD, World Bank and IFC, the notion of a development bank for the Middle East should be proceeded with with great caution. It, as well as any similar political economic institution, must be imbued with a set of ideas that are not based on compromise or 'fudging', but consensus insofar as all the member-states will be able to agree on its overall ideas-based direction. It must be an institution imbued with a set of ideas, coupled with processes and capabilities, that will allow it to put to good use these processes and capabilities for the benefit of the member-states in need. There is already some hesitancy on the part of some of the major donors and the possibility of a clash of goals – a catalyst for private enterprise, or the use of 'soft loans' for infrastructure/developmental projects. Thus unless the 'ideas' of the Middle East development bank are worked out properly and sufficiently, then the possibility of a replication of the problems that have plagued the EBRD since its inception may occur, albeit in the Middle East, with disastrous consequences for the prospects of the building of a 'new Middle East'.[113] Thus the lessons derived from an examination of the EBRD could have a direct bearing on another new institution, and an area of the world undergoing immense and important changes, politically and economically.

Conclusions

The above section illustrates a number of clear and useful points concerning the application of theory and institution building in general. First and foremost, it has made it clear that, with respect to a better and more comprehensive understanding of the workings of the EBRD, an alternative, more critical approach is both warranted and needed. However, the above section also illustrates that an alternative approach that does not concern itself with 'ideas' is not enough. This is why the Coxian paradigm is so useful. It not only takes account of institutional processes and material capabilities from an alternative approach, but combines these factors with 'ideas', 'ideas' that serve one well in developing a richer and more comprehensive understanding of European–US relations within the context of the EBRD.

Second, this application of an 'ideas-based' paradigm has interesting and important implications not only for the future of the EBRD, but also for other political economic institutions, such as the IMF, World Bank and IFC. Most importantly, there are implications to be found with respect to institution building for the future. Given that there is talk of a multilateral developmental bank for the Middle East, politicians and negotiators would be well advised to consider the lessons learned from the experience of the EBRD. However, these lessons will be learned only if the politicians are open and cognizant of the important role that 'ideas' can and will play in the creation and day-to-day management of a development bank. Thus even prior to the setting out of a number of final concluding remarks, which will take place in the next and final chapter, a number of implications – many of a practical nature – can already be highlighted through our use of not only an alternative theoretical paradigm, but a paradigm that is 'ideas based' and critical in orientation.

Notes

1 P. Haas, 'Introduction: knowledge, power and international policy co-ordination', *International Organization*, Vol. 46, No. 1, 1992, p. 7.

2 J. Mearsheimer, 'A realist reply', *International Organization*, Vol. 20, No. 1, 1995; see also his 'The false promise of international institutions', *International Security*, Vol. 19, No. 4, 1994/5, p. 38.

3 Mearsheimer, 'Realist reply', p. 40.

4 M. Neufeld, 'Reflexivity and international relations theory', *Millennium*, Vol. 22, No. 1, 1993, p. 54.

5 *Ibid.*, p. 55.

6 R. Cox, 'Social forces, states and world orders: beyond international relations theory', in R. Keohane (ed.), *Neorealism and its critics*, New York: Columbia University Press, 1986, p. 208. See also pp. 208–9.

7 Neufeld, 'Reflexivity', pp. 72–5.

8 For postmodernist work see R. K. Ashley, 'The geopolitics of geopolitical space', *Alternatives*, Vol. 12, No. 4, 1987; R. K. Ashley and R. B. J. Walker, 'Reading dissidence/writing the discipline', *International Studies Quarterly*, Vol. 34, No. 3, 1990; J. George and D. Campbell, 'Pattern of dissent and the celebration of difference: critical social theory and international relations', *International Studies Quarterly*, Vol. 34, No. 3, 1990; J. Der Derian and M. Shapiro, *International/intertextual relations*, Lexington, Mass.: Lexington Books, 1989; D. Campbell, *Writing security*, Manchester: Manchester University Press, 1992.

9 C. Boggs, *Gramsci's Marxism*, New York: Pluto Press, 1976, p. 39, emphasis added.

10 R. Cox, 'Gramsci, hegemony and international relations: an essay in method', *Millennium*, Vol. 12, No. 2, 1983, p. 168.

11 Cox, 'Social forces', p. 224.

12 *Ibid.*

13 M. Hoffman, 'Critical theory and the inter-paradigm debate', *Millennium*, Vol. 16, No. 2, 1987, p. 231.

14 *Ibid.*, p. 233.

15 K. Waltz, *Theory of international politics*, Reading, Mass.: Addison-Wesley, 1979.

16 R. Keohane (ed.), *Neorealism and its critics*, New York: Columbia University Press, 1986 – and chapters therein by R. Cox, 'Social forces, states and world orders: beyond international relations theory' and by R. K. Ashley, 'The poverty of neorealism'.

17 Hoffman, 'Critical theory', pp. 236–7.

18 *Ibid.*, pp. 237–8.

19 *Ibid.*, pp. 240–3.

20 N. Rengger, 'Going critical? A response to Hoffman', *Millennium*, Vol. 17, No. 1, 1988, p. 86.

21 *Ibid.*

22 *Ibid.*, pp. 81–2, for all three comments.

23 M. Oakeshott, 'Rationalism in politics', in M. Oakeshott (ed.), *Rationalism in politics*, London: Methuen, 1962.

24 Rengger, 'Going critical?', p. 83.

25 *Ibid.*, pp. 83–4.

26 *Ibid.*, p. 83.

27 Mearsheimer, 'False promise', p. 42. This criticism extends to theorists such as Richard Ashley and his 'Poverty of neorealism'.

28 *Ibid.*, pp. 42–3.

29 *Ibid.*, p. 42.

30 *Ibid.*, pp. 45–6.

31 *Ibid.*, p. 46.

32 R. Germain and M. Kenny, 'Engaging Gramsci: IR theory and the new Gramscians', unpublished paper, ISA conference, University of Toronto, Canada, 18–22 March 1997, p. 3.

33 *Ibid.*

34 *Ibid.*, p. 4.

35 *Ibid.*, pp. 11–12.

36 *Ibid.*, p. 23.

37 *Ibid.*, p. 24.

38 *Ibid.*, pp. 28–30.

39 *Ibid.*, pp. 29–30.

40 P. Burnham, 'Neo-Gramscian hegemony and the international order', *Capital and Class*, No. 45, 1991, p. 77.

41 *Ibid.*, pp. 77–9.

42 *Ibid.*, p. 80.

43 *Ibid.*, p. 81.

44 *Ibid.*, p. 84.

45 *Ibid.*, p. 86.

46 Cox, 'Social forces', pp. 223 and 225.

47 Burnham, 'Neo-Gramscian hegemony', p. 90.

48 Mearsheimer, 'False promise', p. 37.

49 Cox, 'Social forces', p. 210.

50 Mearsheimer, 'False promise', p. 38.

51 *Ibid.*, fn. 133.

52 *Ibid.*, p. 38.

53 *Ibid.*, p. 37. Mearsheimer cites as key critical theoretical texts three by Ruggie and another three by Wendt, along with two by Kratochwil. Wendt, in a number of his articles, suggests a return to a 'scientific' brand of realism (e.g. 'The agent–structure problem in international relations theory', *International Organization*, Vol. 41, No. 3, 1987, pp. 369–70), whereas Kratochwil critiques Ashley's criticism of neorealism in his article 'Errors have their advantages', *International Organization*, Vol. 38, No. 2, 1984.

54 Rengger, 'Going critical?', p. 84.

55 Ashley, 'Poverty of neorealism', cited in Mearsheimer, 'False promise', p. 41.

56 A. Bieler, 'Neo-Gramscian approaches to IR theory and the role of ideas: a

response to open Marxism', unpublished paper, BISA conference, University of Durham, 16–18 December 1996.

57 Burnham, 'Neo-Gramscian hegemony', p. 77.

58 *Ibid.*, p. 79.

59 *Ibid.*, emphasis added.

60 *Ibid.*, p. 84.

61 A. Gramsci, *Selections from the prison notebooks*, New York: International Publishers, 1971 (translated by Q. Hoare and G. Nowell Smith), p. 133.

62 *Ibid.*, pp. 175–85, especially 178. See also p. 165.

63 *Ibid.*, p. 184.

64 *Ibid.*, pp. 381–472. Many of the 'problems' of Marxism that are mentioned by Gramsci are those of a 'scientific' and 'objective' nature, again illustrating his *lack* of interest in a structuralist approach to Marxism, yet still desiring to adhere to a form of Marxist thought.

65 Cox, 'Social forces', pp. 205–6 and 214–17.

66 *Ibid.*, p. 221.

67 Cox, *Power, production and world order*, New York: Columbia University Press, 1987, p. ix. Cox is insistent and goes to great lengths in being clear in the use of this term, in that he distinguishes himself by seeking to explore the *mode of social relations of production* rather than only the *mode of production*. This difference goes to the heart of the assertion of this author of a Gramscian approach to 'production' quite at odds from classical Marxist, pluralist and neorealist interpretations.

68 *Ibid.*, p. 1.

69 *Ibid.*, p. 17.

70 Cox states that 'participants in a mode of social relations of production share a mental picture of the mode of ideas of what is normal … and in how people should arrange their lives', *ibid.*, p. 22. See also pp. 22–6, where he defines rationalities as 'coherently worked out patterns of thought'.

71 *Ibid.*, p. 29.

72 A. Wendt, 'Collective identity formation and the international state', *American Political Science Review*, Vol. 88, No. 2, 1994.

73 *Ibid.*, p. 385.

74 *Ibid.*, p. 389.

75 *Ibid.*, p. 394.

76 T. Risse-Kappen, *Cooperation among democracies*, Princeton: Princeton University Press, 1995, p. 3. Risse-Kappen also notes similar works, such as that by Keohane and Goldstein, Peter Haas (mentioned later) and works by Kathryn Sikkink, John Odell and Ernst Haas.

77 *Ibid.*, pp. 4–5.

78 *Ibid.*, p. 31.

79 *Ibid.*, p. 34.

80 *Ibid.*, p. 218.

81 R. Keohane and J. Goldstein, *Ideas and foreign policy*, London: Cornell University Press, 1993, p. 3.

82 *Ibid.*, pp. 8–11.

83 *Ibid.*, pp. 7–8.

84 Risse-Kappen, *Cooperation among democracies*, p. 25.

85 S. Krasner, 'Structural causes and regime consequences', *International Organization*, Vol. 36, No. 2, 1982, p. 186. That special issue of the journal is dedicated to the analysis of regimes and regime theory.

86 Keohane and Goldstein, *Ideas and foreign policy*, p. 3.

87 It is not surprising then that the chapter on his work is entitled 'John G. Ruggie: tranformation and institutionalization'. See O. Waever (ed.), *The future of international relations: masters in the making*, London: Routledge, 1997.

88 J. G. Ruggie, 'Territoriality and beyond: problematizing modernity in international relations', *International Organization*, Vol. 47, No. 1, 1993, p. 173.

89 *Ibid.*, p. 171. See also fn. 140. See more on the rationalist aspects of Wendt's constructivist approach below.

90 *Ibid.*, p. 172.

91 *Ibid.*, p. 174.

92 Keohane and Goldstein, *Ideas and foreign policy*, p. 8.

93 *Ibid.*, see pp. 6–7 and 5.

94 *Ibid.*, p. 11. See also P. Haas (ed.), *Knowledge, power and international policy coordinatioon*, special issue of *International Organization*, Vol. 46, No. 1, 1992.

95 E. Ringmar, 'Alexander Wendt: a social scientist struggling with history', in I. Neumann (ed.), *Masters in the Making*, London: Routledge, 1997, pp. 277–8.

96 *Ibid.*, p. 278.

97 *Ibid.*, p. 279.

98 S. Weber, 'Origins of the European Bank for Reconstruction and Development', *International Organization*, Vol. 48, No. 1, 1994, p. 33.

99 *Ibid.*, p. 34.

100 G. Gallarotti, 'The limits of international organization', *International Organization*, Vol. 45, No. 2, 1991, pp. 192–3.

101 J. Garten, *A cold peace*, New York: Times Books, 1992, p. 119.

102 *Ibid.*, p. 121. See also L. Thurow, *Head to head*, New York: William Morrow Ltd, 1992, especially pp. 32–7.

103 EBRD, personal interviews, 1992.

104 Gallarotti, 'The limits of international organization', pp. 211–18.

105 R. Keohane and J. Nye, *Power and interdependence*, Boston: Little, Brown, 1977, p. 274.

106 Weber, 'Origins', p. 38.

107 Cox, 'Social forces', pp. 208–9.

108 See articles about this reassessment period in *FT*, 21 June 1994, 28 June 1994

and 8 July 1994; *The Guardian*, 18–19 July 1994; *The European*, 15–21 July 1994.

109 J. G. Ruggie, 'International regimes, transactions and change: embedded liberalism in the post-war economic system', *International Organization*, Vol. 36, No. 2, 1982. See also R. Keohane, *After hegemony: cooperation and discord in the world political economy*, Princeton: Princeton University Press, 1984.

110 'Middle East bank key for US', *The Guardian*, 26 October 1994, p. 22.

111 *Ibid.*

112 *Ibid.*

113 Mitterrand's postulation that the work of the EBRD would assist in building a 'united Europe', underpinning the transition to market economies and democracies, at the signing of the charter of the EBRD sound very much like Christopher's call for a 'new Middle East'. Given the troubles of the EBRD since its inception, alarm bells should be sounding in the offices of the politicians interested in establishing a similar institution for the Middle East.

6

A concluding tale:
the fate of the EBRD

Introduction

The creation of a new Europe in the aftermath of the collapse of
the Soviet system of satellite countries, to say nothing of the
failure of Communism, reflects the interests and desires of the
political leadership of Western Europe and North America from
the 1940s. For this reason, the context of the reconstruction of
Europe from 1945 onwards was given at the outset of this case
study of the EBRD. It is well documented by Milward that
disagreements were rife between the United States and its
European allies with respect to the nature and direction of a
recovery programme, in particular with regard to Marshall aid
and the OEEC.[1] While some authors play down these disagreements for the sake of an harmonious picture, there is little
doubt that differences appeared from beginning to end. But, and
one could debate this for many years to come, the Marshall Plan
was not only announced but developed, insofar as monies were
dispersed, plans drawn up and an atmosphere of cooperation
between states (old rivals in some instances) was encouraged.
From this encouragement and cooperation other agreements
flowed, such as the EPU, the ECSC and the EEC and its present-
day version, the EU, where old enemies such as France and

Germany are new and (presumably) long-lasting friends. It was, as Walter Rostow contends, not only a plan to reconstruct Western Europe economically, but to 'create a world unlike that of the failed inter-war years … it was the matrix within which the Europeans drew together and learned from a parochial past. This is indeed a story from which the world can garner a few lessons.'[2]

The EBRD was touted by President Mitterrand as a similar device to the Marshall Plan. The CEECs had been recently freed from the grips of the Soviet Union, and if the West wanted to build a new Europe it had to be prepared not only to encourage such change, but also fund it – hence the creation of the EBRD and its initial allocation, and the excitement generated by the activity emanating from its many floors. However, the context in which the EBRD was founded was also one that generated disagreements over economic and fiscal policies between the allies. It is because of these disagreements, and the redirection of the institution after its first two years of operation, that there is concern that the EBRD, as the sole lending institution dedicated to the transformation of Central and Eastern Europe, will turn out to be even worse than the Marshall Plan with respect to its inability to effect change in countries outside of Central Europe. These disagreements affect not only day-to-day policy, but also comprise a battle of economic and political philosophies. Ideas not only count, but are inherently important in the creation and maintenance of institutions, organizations and regimes alike. This is illustrated by an analysis of the problems associated with the EBRD throughout its existence, and indeed by similar problems with the Marshall Plan. Not only were there problems concerning the structure of the institution, but also with respect to the 'social purpose' of the EBRD. While the former can be solved by reorganization, the latter cannot because these concern the strongly held beliefs of the actors involved.

Questions – the initial years

It is because of these strongly held beliefs on the part of the various Western states that, when the creation of a new institution is being mooted, a specific set of questions must be asked. These include, above all else:

1 Is the disorder that is present in the area of concern likely to increase through the absence of a managed organization?
2 Is there the presence of imperfect and asymmetrical knowledge, risk, uncertainty and irresponsibility and, if so, can an institution reduce these costs?
3 Why are we contemplating an organization – is it in response to the 'do something' syndrome or because of a desire to be economically efficient?
4 Are there a sufficient number of ideas that are fundamental and congruently held among the dominant member-states of the proposed institution?

Based upon the experience of the EBRD, this author would make the claim that the third and fourth questions are the most important, for if there is a lack of congruency between possible member-states, then the establishment of a formal institution may not be the optimum action to take. The experience of the post-1945 period may serve as a lesson in this instance. Rather than creating a formal structure such as the EBRD, the United States and its Western European allies opted for a more informal arrangement by way of the ERP. The ERP was created with the single intention of assisting the recovery of the states of Western Europe, and when this task was accomplished, the ERP was dismantled. While there are differences between 1945 and 1989 in that the ERP was funded solely by the United States, it was still a programme that was decided upon by all the countries involved. Therefore this question of whether or not a congruency in 'ideas' is present or not was still pertinent. Thus lessons can be drawn from the post-1945 world for a better understanding of the world from 1989 onwards.

A second reason to establish a more informal institution would be when the creation of the institution was driven more by a sense of public relations and the need to be seen to be 'doing something'. In this instance, the organization may be fraught by ideas-based divergence that will not subside after the completion of initial negotiations. In fact, if the experience of the Marshall Plan should have taught the politicians who designed the EBRD anything, it is that ideas-based differences were bound to appear within the context of the formative stages of the EBRD and would reappear at a later juncture, not only because they 'count', but because they were initially pushed aside or ignored.

Once these two questions have been asked, only then can others be addressed, with a view to creating a structure that will optimally serve the interests of all of its member-states. Again, the fact that the United States and its European allies decided not to create a formal institution to aid recovery after World War Two, even though they appeared to agree on the fundamental objectives and elements of an economic system, is telling in itself. Given that there were calls for a type of Marshall Plan on the part of the West after 1989, one would have hoped that the politicians would have returned, as this study has, to the post-war period and asked these questions concerning economic and political assistance to Central and Eastern Europe. Quite possibly they may have decided to 'do something', albeit in a different and possibly less formal manner, as was the case with the ERP.

Questions – the post-1992 era

The answers to the above questions, however, relate specifically and only to the pre-1992 phase of the EBRD – the negotiations and first two years of its operations, when it was plagued with disagreement and criticism. They do not, however, address issues relevant to the post-1992 phase at the EBRD, where there was cooperation between the member-states. To this end, another set of questions arise, with their own set of answers and implications, practical as well as theoretical. The three main questions arising from this post-1992 phase are:

1   Did the member-states of the EBRD learn to cooperate?
2   If they did not learn to do so, then what are the implications for the EBRD and the recipient countries of Central and Eastern Europe?
3   What are the theoretical implications for mainstream/traditional theories of cooperation given the above findings?

Not learning to cooperate

The resurgence of the restructuring/privatization debate between member-states of the EBRD is indicative of the lack of substantial cooperation between these countries. The treading of a fine line between what and what may not be defined as a 'market' is a second but nonetheless crucial indicator of this lack of substantial cooperation. The new lending guidelines following the strategic review were the third, final, and possibly most damning indicators of a lack of any meaningful cooperation between the dominant member-states of the EBRD. These three points of reference are important because many of these are elements of debates that are at the heart of what the EBRD may, or may not, be allowed to do in the future with respect to its assistance of the process of transformation in Central and Eastern Europe.

Concentrating on these three issues is not to demean the cooperation that did occur. Certainly, it was in the interest of all the concerned parties to hold a strategic review and appoint a new President who had had experience of international lending. It was also in the interest of all concerned to proceed with a significant restructuring of the decision-making and project-approval procedures of the institution. Not only for the sake of the reputation of the organization was this restructuring necessary, but also for the benefit of the transformation process in Central and Eastern Europe. The ability, now, to direct one's attention to a country unit is seen as beneficial by all the personnel of the EBRD.

However, on those issues that concern the overall, rather than day-to-day, goals and objectives of the Bank, it is apparent that substantial and meaningful cooperation is lacking. The implications of this assessment of member-state relations within the EBRD are important for both the institution itself and its recipient countries. First and foremost, the EBRD will continue to lurch from one point of contention to another because of this lack of ideas-based cooperation. Worse, the Bank will not be able to develop to its fullest potential because these issues are not new ones. The proof of a lack of ideas-based cooperation is that old issues have re-emerged because, rather than in spite of, a lack of cooperation. Had the member-states made it a point to debate and negotiate in good faith, many of these points of contention would have not resurfaced. Instead, positions were compromised without a final settlement being agreed to. Everyone received something, while the staff of the institution received nothing but differing and at times conflicting guidelines to follow. The new strategic guidelines are a prime example of this desire for compromise as a means of avoiding debate and settlement. The Anglo-Saxon countries got 'sound banking' and 'transition impact' while the continental Europeans were handed 'conditionality'. Even senior management and directors agree that the first two principles are at odds with the third.

The EBRD and its recipient countries

A number of the recipient countries of the EBRD such as Poland, Hungary, Slovakia and the Czech Republic are bound to graduate from this status in the near future. With membership of both NATO and the EU assured since the relevant pronouncements in 1997, these four states will attain greater access to EU funds and therefore become less dependent, if at all, on EBRD capital for their economic transformation. However, this prospect of graduation for Central Europe says nothing of the continuing plight of the states that may not become EU members for quite some time, if at all in the case of some of the more eastern countries of the region and the former republics of the Soviet Union. Therefore after graduation takes places, some countries will remain behind for the foreseeable future and require even more assistance from the EBRD in order to attain a transitional state equal to that of the Polands and Hungarys of Central Europe. However, because of the new self-imposed conditions under which the EBRD Board of Governors operates, the profit requirement that merchant banks insist upon, and the demands of other in-need and emergency areas of the world that are placed upon the World Bank and IMF, the EBRD may find itself without a role in the parts of Eastern Europe where it is required the most with respect to political and economic transformation. The irony will become that the institution that was created to merge East with West, and hailed as the start of a 'great' Europe, will soon find itself without employment because of its own criteria, rather than a lack of need or opportunity. Instead, the EBRD will be without a role because it will be compromised out of such a role by the lack of substantial and meaningful agreement between the dominant donor states of the organization.

The evidence for such a conclusion is found in the documents of the EBRD. The tables in Appendix G illustrate, on one hand, the growth of the number of projects that the EBRD has become involved in since 1991. From a low of 30 to a high of 109 in 1995, the Bank has become very active throughout Central and Eastern Europe and the former Soviet Union. Its concentration, per se, on the countries of Eastern Europe has also grown since its inception. From ten agreed projects in 1991, the EBRD was involved in the disbursement of loans or took a share of sixty-six and sixty projects in 1995 and 1996, respectively. In terms of monetary sums, this increase in the number of projects has also led to an increase in funds dispersed by almost 2 billion ECU from 1991 through to 1996. But there is another story that is also told by these same figures. The tables have been split up into three country areas – Central Europe (Poland, Hungary, Czech Republic, Slovakia), Russia (Russian Federation only) and Other, which includes the other eighteen countries vying for economic assist-ance. On this basis, these 'Other' countries each received, over a six-year period, more than 300 million ECU *less* than those of Central Europe, and in no year save for 1997, which is incomplete in its data, did any of these countries receive monies anywhere close to the amounts received by each of the four of Central Europe. As predicted above, the principles of sound banking and transition impact appear to have affected the region in the manner in which staff at the EBRD, as well as this author and other experts, have concluded. Even in the two last years of complete evidence (1995 and 1996), the countries most in need of assistance each received, on average, 60 million and 30 million ECU less than each of the four countries located in Central Europe. If these four are on the verge of graduation and EU membership, they do not need the assistance of the EBRD on the level that has been given. And yet they continue to do so, in spite of the fact that the countries of Eastern Europe, those with no possibility of either graduation or EU membership, receive much less. It is true that the figures have declined for the former, and risen for the latter over the course of six years, but if the EBRD is to make a difference in the areas in which it is truly needed, then the tables must represent even greater change in programme direction than the figures indicate. If it does not (and the 1997 figures were not complete at the time of writing) then, as stated above, the EBRD will become meaningless to the countries in need that it was created to assist, and the West will have surely made one more move in the direction of losing the peace it so long fought for during the long years of the Cold War.

The EBRD and its donor countries

Of course, the donor countries will not suffer because of the relative demise of the EBRD. Instead, it will be those countries that can afford failure the least, as it often is when Western states fail to agree and cooperate. Most areas of the world have, or are in the process of attaining, a regional development bank. As discussed at the end of the last chapter, a core aspect of the rejuvenation of the Middle East in the wake of the peace process of the mid-1990s may be the creation of a Middle Eastern development bank of some sort. The potential long-term benefits of such a bank, funded by Western states to assist in the economic and social development of poor and underdeveloped Middle Eastern states, are obvious. The results can already be seen in South East Asia with the Asian Development Bank. The EBRD was supposed to act in the same manner as that Bank and, more importantly, the Marshall Plan, where the leadership of one country agreed that it was in its own interests financially to assist the political, economic and military reconstruction of the countries of Western Europe. Therefore it was to be a bank designed for the specific, overarching and obvious needs of the CEECs. Where few countries on their own would not act, because of the risks entailed, or could not act, because of the lack of capital required, the EBRD could act. Because private firms did not want to lend and merchant banks were uninterested or non-existent, the European Bank had to lend. Thus a lifeline of less than epic proportions was thrown to these countries in their desire to transform themselves from Communist command economic and political structures to Western-styled democracies and market-based economies. And the benefits of the EBRD can be seen in the most developed and transformed of these economies. In effect, in some of these countries the EBRD has put itself out of employment – a development which should be seen as a good thing and a credit to the entire staff of the institution.

But there are still countries that will, for the foreseeable future, require the services of an institution that is able and supposed to assist where others will not. In countries such as Albania merchant banks and foreign companies are not prepared to take risks of such magnitude with the capital of their shareholders. Given the state of these economies, not to mention those of Western states, no one of the latter is prepared to grant such sums of capital to one country or another. The World Bank will assist, but its remit is global. The demands on its pools of capital are, therefore, greater than just Central and Eastern Europe (see Appendix H).[3] With countries in Africa, for example, still requiring massive assistance, the attention of these international bodies is and will remain divided. Thus those countries of Eastern Europe that require immediate, long-term, lengthy and devoted attention will not receive it if the current status of the EBRD is not resolved, one way or another. In the end, if ideas-based cooperation is not achieved at the EBRD, then the poorest of the poor and the weakest of the weak will suffer.

However, if long-term security, both political and economic, rests with the transformation of Central *and* Eastern Europe, then the poorest and weakest will not be the only ones to lose out. Immediately, the states of Central Europe will not receive the benefits of neighbouring states that have developing or developed trading economies. Goods will not be bought, economies will not grow and political processes may remain underdeveloped. All of these potential occurrences may lead to political unrest, upheaval, a return to nationalism or authoritarianism, or other non-democratic forms of governance. In turn, the security of this area of the world – Central and Eastern Europe – may be placed in doubt. If the long-term security of *Western* Europe rests upon the stability of this other half of the continent, then the entirety of Europe would suffer because of the inability of the donor member-states of the EBRD to cooperate in a meaningful manner.

The above is obviously an extreme scenario of what could happen if the key lending facility for Central and Eastern Europe becomes a marginal actor in the process of transformation. But this scenario may also not be far from the truth. If the politics of Russia is anything to go by, then the return of nationalism, racism, authoritarianism and other non-democratic forms of governance, along with massive corruption and the growth of organized crime, is not far-fetched. Already, economists are blaming the West for the return of Communists and the nationalist rantings of the Liberal Democrats because of its stringent loan conditions and slowness in the disbursement of IMF and World Bank funds. Could not the same occur in Eastern Europe?

Whether or not the Marshall Plan was a success, or even an unmitigated failure as Alan Milward contends,[4] there is a truism to the project that cannot be denied. There was something unique about one country, and in particular General Marshall, who decided that the United States should commit itself to the funding of a massive assistance package to Western Europe. Certainly there were conditions attached to these funds, and most likely an oversimplification of the problems of the region by US officials that was coupled with an ideological bent towards open markets rather than protectionist cartels, but these issues still do not denigrate the commitment that the United States expressed in its desire not to 'lose the peace' after fighting so hard to 'win the war'. A post-war settlement that would have left Europe open to, again, nationalism, militarism, aggressive chauvinism and economic protectionism was not what was in the best interests of Europe or the United States, and the latter acted in order to prevent what occurred in the inter-war period because of the absence of strong leadership and a strong institutional framework guaranteed by a country (or set of countries) that would be able to underwrite the costs of such a project. This is not to say that there was an absence of disagreement between the parties involved, because Milward and other scholars make it clear that such disagreements, and fundamental ones at that with respect to political economic priorities, were present throughout the reconstruction period. However, even in the face of these differences, the leadership of the United States and its Western European allies were able to compromise their ideas so that Europe could be reconstructed. This meant that Western European states had to agree to work together in order to access Marshall Plan capital, and the United States supported projects such as the ECSC even if its leadership saw this as a project that ran contrary to its own economic philosophy regarding open markets. The call by leading central bankers such as Duisenberg for a new Marshall Plan, given the tangible and intangible benefits derived from the commitment itself, is perfectly understandable. What is not, by and large, is the reaction on the part of the states of Western Europe and the United States. A refusal to learn the lessons of the past, and a lack of interest in tackling ideas-based concerns in the formative years of the EBRD, combined with the absence of a real sense of obligation and concern for the future of Eastern Europe, has delivered the EBRD and its members to the situation it finds itself in today – one of potential irrelevance in the wake of a massive and quite real need for economic assistance of an unqualified and unconditional nature.

The EBRD and international relations theory

The third and final implication of the lack of ideas-based cooperation between EBRD member-states is theoretical in nature. As mentioned previously, theories of cooperation derived from traditional theories of international relations are inherently weak in explaining this phenomenon. While able to describe aspects or elements of cooperative behaviour, the fundamental weaknesses of the EBRD lay uncovered by an inability of any of these paradigms to discover, describe, explain and understand the whole beast. By not being inclusive of 'ideas' alongside other factors, such as material capabilities and institutional processes, these traditional theories lack the power to develop a more complex and useful understanding of other terms of reference such as hegemony, not to mention the everyday workings of the EBRD. These weaknesses are highlighted and compounded by the presence of a theoretical tradition that is able to achieve some measure of 'success' in all three areas of concern. Robert Cox's Gramscian-inspired variant of Marxist thought is, first and foremost, able to be inclusive of ideas while not excluding state behaviour, institutional processes, and understanding of national self-interest and the value of material capabilities.

Second, this analysis is able to step back from the world as it is and assess the whole and the parts, rather than only the parts. While not without flaws and its own blind spots, this approach is able to perform that task asked of, but not delivered by, traditional theories of inter-state cooperation.

Third, and finally, because of its interest in 'ideas', this perspective is able to examine more than already meets the eye with respect to the degree of cooperation being undertaken by the member-states of the EBRD. More than simply stating that this lack of cooperation is ideas and materially based, this Coxian analysis is able to proceed one step further in its understanding of EBRD practices and, by inference, implications for member-states and recipient countries. The present partially successful attempt by Anglo-Saxon countries to usurp the ideas-based control of the EBRD by continental European countries and replace this with an Anglo-Saxon variant is nothing more than the age-old attempt to replace one hegemonic order with another. Confusion, uncertainty and instability reign while opposing forces battle for the control of a given thing. In this instance the 'thing' is the EBRD. Such an analysis, one that may strike at the heart of the problems one may and can associate with the EBRD, may not be able to be achieved by traditional theories of inter-state relations.

The larger implication is not only that a Coxian analysis should be continually applied to the EBRD, but that when assessing cooperation alternative theoretical positions should not be dismissed out of hand, as was done by John Mearsheimer.[5] Not only was his depiction of critical theory biased and incorrect, but a possible sign of fear that this perspective could be very useful in explaining and understanding if given half the chance to do so. Also, by doing such an injustice, Mearsheimer has weakened whatever credibility the neorealist movement had with respect to its validity and status as *the* theory of international relations. Given that this book has, in its application of the Coxian Gramscian analysis, gone past the initial use of 'ideas' to describe hegemony, the indication is that little by little we are able to fashion a truly comprehensive understanding of international relations between states that is not dependent upon a traditional/mainstream/realist-based reading of these relations. The implication is that critical theory, whether it is a Gramscian or postmodern approach, has something valuable to say concerning issues that are directly and indirectly related to matters of war and peace, broadly *or* narrowly defined. To this end, it should be allowed, and for the sake of the state of the discipline, encouraged to speak its mind without the interruptions presented by Mearsheimer.

Final remarks

The Marshall Plan, faults and all, was a commitment to assist in the political and economic reconstruction of Western Europe. Disagreements between the donor country and its partners were present through these years, yet agreements on convertibility, a payments union, trading networks and projects to revive specific industries were made for the overall benefit of both the donor and recipient countries. The EBRD has been, is and will likely be in the future beset with a similar range of disagreements concerning similar political economic ideas and ideologies. However, the presence of an utter lack of meaningful and substantive cooperation between its member-states is in glaring contrast to the post-1945 period of reconstruction. Like that period, this lack of cooperation arose not only because of practical, pragmatic and political considerations, but also because of large differences with respect to 'ideas', and on what principles the EBRD should be based and administered. However, it is only through a more critical analysis that such an understanding can be derived, simultaneously illustrating the strength of this approach and the weaknesses of those of a traditional nature. It is the hope of this author that this book will stimulate more debate concerning the future of the EBRD, the plight of the recipient countries in need and the fate of similar political economic organizations (existing and in the planning stages). Finally, it is also the hope of the author that this book will draw further attention to the realm of possibilities obtainable through a critical, rather than traditional, investigation of the world of inter-state relations.

Notes

1 A. Milward, *The reconstruction of Western Europe 1945–51*, London: Methuen, 1984.
2 W. Rostow, 'Lessons of the Plan', *Foreign Affairs*, Vol. 76, No. 3, 1997, p. 204.
3 Figures in Appendix H from the World Bank are telling to two ways. The first is that, as with the EBRD, the flow of capital to Central and Eastern Europe has been and remains imbalanced massively towards the four primary states of Central Europe. The difference per country is over $1.2 billion with respect to what the former receive in comparison with the states of Eastern Europe and the former Soviet republics. Second, capital flows to the European continent (primarily Central and Eastern Europe) accounted for only 21 per cent of the total aid assistance from 1992 to 1997 from the World Bank. Latin America and the Caribbean and East Asia received, as a percentage, more, and other large transfers were directed to Africa. Thus the EBRD, with its one-dimensional nature, should be able to, and should, do more with respect to these states given the multidimensional nature and interests of its international counterpart agency.
4 Milward, *Reconstruction of Western Europe*.
5 J. Mearsheimer, 'The false promise of international institutions', *International Security*, Vol. 19, No. 4, 1994/5.

Appendix A

Operation PHARE

Operation PHARE – Poland/Hungary Aid for Reconstruction Enterprise, 1989–90 (million ECU)

Country[a]	Farm.	Ind.	Env.	Edu.	Health	Aid	Other	Total
Poland	100	56.0	22.0	16.6				194.6
Hungary	20	35.3	27.0	12.0	3.0			97.3
Bulgaria	16		3.5	4.0	5.0			28.5
Czech Republic			30.0	1.0				31.0
East Germany			20.0				14.0	34.0
Romania					4.4	11.1		15.5
Yugoslavia		35.0						35.0
Other						51.0	12.9	63.9
Total	136	126.3	102.5	33.6	12.4	62.1	26.9	500.0

Farm., farming; Ind., industry; Env., environment; Edu., education.
[a]The programme was almost immediately expanded to the other countries, but kept its original name.

Source: *PHARE scorecard*, G-24 Coordinating Unit, DG for External Affairs, Commission of the EC, 30 January 1991.

Appendix B

Selected EC aid programmes – Central and Eastern Europe

Date	Programme	Comment
9 October 1989	130 million ECU	Poland
9 October 1989	220 million ECU	Poland, Hungary
9 October 1989	1.1 billion ECU	Poland, Hungary loan guarantees
24 September 1990	EC–Bulgaria	Trade, commerce agreements
24 September 1990	EC–Czechoslovakia	Trade, commerce agreements
24 September 1990	EC–Poland	Joint committee meeting[a]
October 1990	EC–Romania	Joint committee meeting
29 October 1990	600 million ECU	Hungary, part of 1 billion ECU loan
12 November 1990	200 million ECU	ECSC loan to Poland
12 November 1990	Energy charter	Central/Eastern Europe energy charter with EC
26–27 November 1990	EC–Hungary	Joint committee meeting
30 November 1990	West Germany–Czechoslovakia	Cooperation treaty
5 December 1990	Italy–Czechoslovakia	Technical agreement
6 December 1990	1.0 billion ECU	G-24–Czechoslovakia

Table continues over

171

Date	Programme	Comment
6 December 1990	0.7 billion ECU	G-24–Hungary
6 December 1990	1.0 billion ECU	G-24–Poland
6 December 1990	7.0 billion ECU	G-24 general fund
26 December 1990	EC Association negotiations	Poland, Hungary, Czech Republic
11 January 1991	514 million ECU	Loan to Czech Republic
29 January 1991	650 million ECU	Hungary, part of 1 billion ECU loan
28 February 1991	930 million ECU	Credits to Romania, Bulgaria, Czech Republic
5 March 1991	France–Czech Republic	Food producer agreement

[a]Meeting of EC and national trade subcommittees to discuss trade and other assistance.
Source: US Foreign Bureau Information Service, various texts.

Appendix C

The EBRD's share/capital subscription investment by member-state, 1990

Country	Capital subscription (million ECU)
Donor countries	
Belgium	228.00
Denmark	120.00
France	851.75
West Germany	851.75
Greece	65.00
Ireland	30.00
Italy	851.75
Luxembourg	20.00
The Netherlands	248.00
Portugal	42.00
Spain	340.00
United Kingdom	851.75
EEC	300.00
European Investment Bank	300.00
Austria	228.00
Cyprus	10.00
Finland	125.00
Iceland	10.00
Israel	65.00
Liechtenstein	2.00
Malta	1.00
Norway	125.00

Table continues over

Country	Capital subscription (million ECU)
Sweden	228.00
Switzerland	228.00
Turkey	115.00
Australia	100.00
Canada	340.00
Egypt	10.00
Japan	851.75
South Korea	65.00
Mexico	3.00
Morocco	10.00
New Zealand	10.00
United States of America	1,000.00
Recipient countries	
Bulgaria	79.00
Czechoslovakia	128.00
East Germany	155.00
Hungary	79.00
Poland	128.00
Soviet Union	600.00
Yugoslavia	128.00
Romania	128.00

Source: EBRD, *Basic documents.*

Appendix D

The EBRD's share/capital subscription investment by member-state, 1999

Country	Capital subscription (million ECU)
Donor countries	
Austria	228.00
Belgium	228.00
Denmark	120.00
Finland	125.00
France	851.75
Germany	851.75
Greece	65.00
Ireland	30.00
Italy	851.75
Luxembourg	20.00
Netherlands	248.00
Portugal	42.00
Spain	340.00
Sweden	228.00
United Kingdom	851.75
European Union	300.00
European Investment Bank	300.00
Total – EU and member-states	*56.16% of total shares*
Cyprus	10.00
Iceland	10.00
Israel	65.00
Liechtenstein	2.00
Malta	1.00

Table continues over

Country	Capital subscription (million ECU)
Norway	125.00
Switzerland	228.00
Turkey	115.00
Australia	100.00
Canada	340.00
Egypt	10.00
Japan	851.75
South Korea	65.00
Mexico	30.00
Morocco	10.00
New Zealand	10.00
United States of America	1,000.00
Recipient countries	
Albania	10.00
Armenia	5.00
Azerbaijan	10.00
Belarus	20.00
Bulgaria	79.00
Croatia	36.46
Czech Republic	85.33
Estonia	10.00
Former Yugoslav Republic of Macedonia	6.91
Georgia	10.00
Hungary	79.00
Kazakhstan	23.00
Kyrgyzstan	10.00
Latvia	10.00
Lithuania	10.00
Moldova	10.00
Poland	128.00
Russian Federation	400.00
Slovak Republic	42.67
Slovenia	20.98
Tajikistan	10.00
Turkmenistan	1.00
Ukraine	80.00
Uzbekistan	21.00
Total – recipient countries	*11.18%*

Source: EBRD, Publications Services, 1996.

Appendix E

The EBRD's charter (selected text)

Article 1 – Purposes

In contributing to economic progress and reconstruction, the purposes of the Bank shall be to foster the transition towards open market-oriented economies and promote private and entrepreneurial initiative in the Central and East European countries committed to and applying the principles of multi-party democracy, pluralism and market economics.

Article 2 – Functions

1. To fulfil on a long-term basis its purposes of fostering the transition of Central and East European countries towards open market-oriented economies and the promotion of private and entrepreneurial initiative, the Bank shall assist the recipient member countries to implement structural and sectoral economic reforms, including demonopolization, decentralization and privatization, to help their economies become fully integrated into the international economy by measures:

(i)   to promote, through private and other interested investors, the establishment, improvement and expansion of productive, competitive and private sector activity, in particular small and medium-sized enterprises;

(ii)   to mobilize domestic and foreign capital and experienced management to the end described in (1);

(iii)   to foster productive investment, including in the service and financial sectors, and in related infrastructure where that is necessary to support private and entrepreneurial initiative, thereby assisting in the making of a competitive environment and raising productivity, the standard of living and conditions of labour;

(iv)   to provide technical assistance for the preparation, financing and implementation of relevant projects, whether individual or in the context of specific investment programmes;

(v)   to stimulate and encourage the development of capital markets;

(vi)   to give support to sound and economically viable projects involving more than one recipient member country;

(vii)   to promote in the full range of its activities environmentally sound and sustainable development; and

(viii) to undertake such other activities and provide such other services as may further these functions.

Source: EBRD, *Basic documents*.

Political mandate of the EBRD (selected text)

Foreword

The Agreement establishing the European Bank for Reconstruction and Development includes a significant political element in that it specifies that the Bank may conduct its operations in countries of Central and Eastern Europe which not only are proceeding in their transition towards market oriented economies, but also are applying principles of multiparty democracy and pluralism....

III. Implementation

A) Objectives

Because of the critical link between the economic and political aspects of the Agreement, the decision on an appropriate way to assess the progress of countries of operation towards multiparty democracy, pluralism and market economies is vital to the Bank's successful fulfilment of its mandate. The specifically economic aspect of the Bank's mandate is outside the scope of this memorandum, but an assessment of economic as well as political factors will be fundamental to an overall view of the implementation of the Bank's purpose in the countries of operation.

In considering how to assess political progress, emphasis is often placed on human rights. References to human rights are in fact found in the Preamble, although not in the Agreement itself. This drafting choice was deliberate. It does not exclude human rights from the scope of the political aspects of the Bank's mandate, but it indicates that only those rights which, in accordance with international standards, are essential elements of multiparty democracy, pluralism, and market economics, should be considered when evaluating a country's progress. Such a reading of the Agreement focuses primarily on civil and political rights. Other rights, including economic and social rights that advance multiparty democracy, pluralism and market economics could be taken into account and fostered by the Bank in connection with its normal operations.

B) Procedures

Against that background, and that of the experience of other relevant institutions, it seems appropriate to assess political and economic progress together, annually, in the bank's country strategy papers, rather than on a project by project basis. The approach to the assessment might considered progress on factors relevant to the political aspects of the Bank's purpose, as set out in Article 1, drawn from the various reference points cited in Section II above, eg:

- free elections;
- representative government in which the executive is accountable to the elected legislature or the electorate;
- duty of the government and the public authorities to act in accordance with the constitution and law, and availability of redress against administrative decisions;
- separation between the State and political parties;
- independence of the judiciary;
- equal protection under the law, including for minorities;
- fair criminal procedure;
- freedom of speech, including the media, of association, and of peaceful assembly;
- freedom of conscience and religion;
- freedom of movement;
- the right to private property; and
- the right to form trade unions and to strike.

If the formal assessment of implementation of the political aspects of the Bank's purpose indicate that a country is implementing policies that, to a greater or lesser degree, are inconsistent with that purpose, paragraph 3 of Article 8 provides the Bank's governing bodies ... substantial flexibility in formulating the Bank's response.

... Action by the Board of Governors might include, according to the circumstances:

- recommendations;
- postponement of proposed operations;
- restrictions of operations;
- suspension of operations.

In formulating its response, the Bank might consider curtailing planned public sector projects before taking action on private operations. Within the public sector it might curtail state infrastructure projects before local ones and endeavour to continue with its technical cooperation activities as long as possible.

Source: *Political aspects of the mandate of the European Bank for Reconstruction and Development*, pp. 2, 5–7.

EBRD projects by year and area, 1991–7

In the tables below, Central comprises Poland, Hungary, the Czech Republic and Slovakia; Russia represents the entire Russian Federation; and Other comprises the remaining eighteen EBRD recipient countries (note the four against eighteen comparison of Central with Other).

Source: EBRD, Information Section, 1998.

Total funding (million ECU) of EBRD projects per country, 1991–7

Area	Total	Percentage	Per country
Central	2401.4	26	600.35
Russia	2221.6	24	2221.60
Other	4624.8	50	256.90
Total	9247.8	100	

Number (and percentage of total) of projects

Area	1991–2	1993	1994	1995	1996	1997
Central	18 (60)	34 (52)	27 (29)	25 (23)	19 (18)	3 (10)
Russia	2 (1)	7 (11)	16 (17)	22 (21)	26 (25)	6 (20)
Other	10 (33)	25 (38)	47 (51)	66 (61)	60 (57)	16 (53)
Total	30	66	93	109	106	29

Funds (million ECU) (and percentage of total) for projects

Area	1991–2	1993	1994	1995	1996	1997
Central	225.8 (34)	596.6 (42)	597.9 (32)	521.9 (26)	408.1 (17)	51.1 (7)
Russia	5.9 (–)	305.4 (22)	399.9 (22)	503.6 (25)	762.4 (31)	244.4 (33)
Other	435.8 (65)	516.5 (37)	888.1 (47)	1015.6 (50)	1296.2 (53)	454.6 (61)
Total	667.5	1418.5	1885.9	2041.1	2466.7	750.1

Appendix H

World Bank distribution of funds

By country, 1990–7 ($million)

Area	Amount	Amount per country
Central	7.019	1.754
Other	12.065	548.000

Central comprises Poland Hungary, the Czech Republic and Slovakia; 'Other' comprises Albania, Armenia, Azerbaijan, Belarus, Bosnia, Bulgaria, Croatia, Estonia, Georgia, Kazakhstan, Kyrgyzstan, Latvia, Lithuania, the Former Yugoslav Republic of Macedonia, Moldava, Romania, Slovenia, Tajikistan, Turkmenistan, Ukraine, Uzbekistan, Yugoslavia.

By region ($billion), 1992–7

Area	Amount	% of total
Central and Eastern Europe	23.662	21
Africa	16.360	15
Latin America/Caribbean	31.600	28
Middle East	8.002	7
East Asia	33.031	29
Total	112.655	100

Source: Multiple sites, WWW.WorldBank.Org

Bibliography

Documents

European Bank for Reconstruction and Development

Basic documents of the EBRD, 29 May 1990
Political aspects of the mandate of the EBRD, 1991
Proceedings of the first annual general meeting of the EBRD, April 1991
Blueprint, 18 December 1991; 12 May 1992
Annual general report, March 1992
Proceedings of the second annual general meeting of the EBRD, 13–15 April 1992
Proceedings of the third annual meeting of the Board of Governors, 18–19 April 1994
Proceedings of the annual meeting, 18–19 April 1994
Proceedings of the annual meeting, 10–11 April 1995
Transition reports, 1994 and 1995
Information Office communiqués, 1992; press release, 31 July 1995

Personal interviews were conducted with many directors and staff members at the EBRD over a period of three years (1992–5)

European Community/Union

Official Journal of the European Community, 25 October 1989; 25 December 1989
Bulletin of the European Community, EC–12, 1989

United States Information Service

'US role in Reconstruction Bank reviewed', 28 June 1990
'Declaration on US–EC relations', 23 November 1990
J. Baker, 'Opportunities to build a new world order', 6 February 1991

Books and articles

Acheson, D., *Present at the creation*, London: Weidenfield and Nicolson, 1969

Ashley, R. K., 'The poverty of neorealism', in R. Keohane (ed.), *Neorealism and its critics*, New York: Columbia University Press, 1986

——, 'The geopolitics of geopolitical space', *Alternatives*, Vol. 12, No. 4, 1987

——, Walker, R. B. J., 'Reading dissidence/writing the discipline', *International Studies Quarterly*, Vol. 34, No. 3, 1990

Attali, J., 'Economic implications of transformation in the Soviet Union: what policy options exist?', EBRD, 22 October 1991

Axelrod, R., *The evolution of cooperation*, New York: Basic Books, 1984

Bieler, A., 'Neo-Gramscian approaches to IR theory and the role of ideas: a response to open Marxism', unpublished paper, BISA conference, University of Durham, 16–18 December 1996

Bod, P., 'Financing transition in Central and Eastern Europe: the role of the EBRD in the reconstruction of the region', unpublished EBRD memo, 1996

Boggs, C., *Gramsci's Marxism*, New York: Pluto Press, 1976

Brzezinski, Z., 'For Eastern Europe, a \$25 billion aid package', *New York Times*, 7 March 1990, p. A25

Burnham, P., 'Neo-Gramscian hegemony and the international order', *Capital and Class*, No. 45, 1991

Campbell, D., *Writing security*, Manchester: Manchester University Press, 1992

Cox, R., 'Gramsci, hegemony and international relations: an essay in method', *Millennium*, Vol. 12, No. 2, 1983

——, 'Social forces, states and world orders: beyond international relations theory', in R. Keohane (ed.), *Neorealism and its critics*, New York: Columbia University Press, 1986

——, *Power, production and world order*, New York: Columbia University Press, 1987

De Larosiere, J., Per Jacobsen lecture, EBRD, 29 September 1996

Der Derian, J., Shapiro, M., *International/intertextual relations*, Lexington, Mass.: Lexington Books, 1989

Duisenberg, W., 'Lessons of the Marshall Plan', *European Affairs*, Vol. 5, No. 3, 1991

Gaddis, J., *Strategies of containment*, New York: Oxford University Press, 1982

Gallarotti, G., 'The limits of international organization', *International Organization*, Vol. 45, No. 2, 1991

Garten, J., *A cold peace*, New York: Times Books, 1992

George, J., Campbell, D., 'Pattern of dissent and the celebration of difference: critical social theory and international relations', *International Studies Quarterly*, Vol. 34, No. 3, 1990

Germain R., Kenny, M., 'Engaging Gramsci: IR theory and the new Gramscians', unpublished paper, ISA conference, University of Toronto, Canada, 18–22 March 1997

Gramsci, A., *Selections from the prison notebooks*, New York: International Publishers, 1971 (translated by Q. Hoare and G. Nowell Smith)

Gray, F., 'World Bank approves new co-financing tool', *Financial Times*, 22 November 1991, p. 7

Haas, P., 'Introduction: knowledge, power and international policy coordination', *International Organization*, Vol. 46, No. 1, 1992

——, 'Conclusion: epistemic communities, world order, and the creation of a reflective research program', *International Organization*, Vol. 46, No. 1, 1992

Hoffman, M., 'Critical theory and the inter-paradigm debate', *Millennium*, Vol. 16, No. 2, 1987

Hogan, M., *The Marshall Plan*, Cambridge: Cambridge University Press, 1987

Jervis, R., 'Realism, game theory and cooperation', *World Politics*, Vol. 40, April 1988

Keohane, R., *After hegemony: cooperation and discord in the world political economy*, Princeton: Princeton University Press, 1984

——, 'Achieving cooperation under anarchy: strategies and institutions', *World Politics*, Vol. 38, No. 1, 1985

—— (ed.), *Neorealism and its critics*, New York: Columbia University Press, 1986

——, 'Theory of world politics', in R. Keohane (ed.), *Neorealism and its critics*, New York: Columbia University Press, 1986

——, *International institutions and state power*, Boulder: Westview Press, 1988

——, Goldstein, J., *Ideas and foreign policy*, London: Cornell University Press, 1993

——, Martin, L., 'The promise of institutional theory', *International Security*, Vol. 20, No. 1, 1995

——, Nye, J., *Power and interdependence*, Boston: Little, Brown, 1977

Krasner, S., 'Regimes and the limits of realism: regimes as autonomous variables', *International Organization*, Vol. 36, No. 2, 1982

——, 'Structural causes and regime consequences', *International Organization*, Vol. 36, No. 2, 1982

——, 'Achieving cooperation under anarchy: strategies and institutions', *World Politics*, Vol. 38, No. 1, 1985

Kratochwil, F., 'Errors have their advantages', *International Organization*, Vol. 38, No. 2, 1984

Marjolin, R., *Architect of European unity*, London: Wiedenfeld and Nicolson, 1989

Mearsheimer, J., 'The false promise of international institutions', *International Security*, Vol. 19, No. 4, 1994/5

——, 'A realist reply', *International Organization*, Vol. 20, No. 1, 1995

Mendelson, S., 'Internal battles and external wars', *World Politics*, Vol. 45, No. 3, 1993

Menkveld, P., *Origin and role of the European Bank for Reconstruction and Development*, London: Graham and Trotman, 1992

Milward, A., *The reconstruction of Western Europe 1945–51*, London: Methuen, 1984

Neufeld, M., 'Reflexivity and international relations theory', *Millennium*, Vol. 22, No. 1, 1993

Oakeshott, M., 'Rationalism in politics', in M. Oakeshott (ed.), *Rationalism in politics*, London: Methuen, 1962

Oye, K., 'Explaining cooperation under anarchy', *World Politics*, Vol. 38, No. 1, 1985

Price, H., *The Marshall Plan and its meaning*, Ithaca: Cornell University Press, 1955

Puchala, D., 'Of blind men, elephants and internal integration', *Journal of Common Market Studies*, Vol. 10, No. 3, 1972

Rengger, N., 'Going critical? A response to Hoffman', *Millennium*, Vol. 17, No. 1, 1988

Ringmar, E., 'Alexander Wendt: a social scientist struggling with history', in I. Neumann (ed.), *Masters in the making*, London: Routledge, 1997

Risse-Kappen, T., 'Ideas do not float freely', *International Organization*, Vol. 48, No. 2, 1994

——, *Cooperation among democracies*, Princeton: Princeton University Press, 1995

Rostow, W., 'Lessons of the plan', *Foreign Affairs*, Vol. 76, No. 3, 1997

Ruggie, J. G., 'International regimes, transactions and change: embedded liberalism in the post-war economic system', *International Organization*, Vol. 36, No. 2, 1982

——, 'Territoriality and beyond: problematizing modernity in international relations', *International Organization*, Vol. 47, No. 1, 1993

——, 'Transformation and institutionalization', in O. Waever (ed.), *The future of international relations: masters in the making*, London: Routledge, 1997

Shihata, I., *The European Bank for Reconstruction and Development*, London: Graham and Trotman, 1990

Thurow, L., *Head to head*, New York: William Morrow, 1992

Waever, O. (ed.), *The future of international relations: masters in the making*, London: Routledge, 1997

Waltz, K., *Theory of international politics*, Reading, Mass.: Addison-Wesley, 1979

Weber, S., 'Origins of the European Bank for Reconstruction and Development', *International Organization*, Vol. 48, No. 1, 1994

Wendt, A., 'The agent–structure problem in international relations theory', *International Organization*, Vol. 41, No. 3, 1987

——, 'Collective identity formation and the international state', *American Political Science Review*, Vol. 88, No. 2, 1994

Wexler, I., *The Marshall Plan revisited*, Westport: Greenwood Press, 1983

Newspapers and magazines

New York Times

'A new bank plans East European aid', 30 May 1990, p. A14
'Industrial nations to create bank to aid Eastern Europe', 10 April 1990, p. D2
See also: 26 March 1990; 13 December 1989

Financial Times

'Bush rejects lending to the Soviet Union', 19 March 1990, p. 2
'Mitterrand says EBRD is step to united Europe', 16 April 1990, p. 1
'US urges World Bank policy shift', 19 April 1991, p. 24
'US supports rise in capital for IFC', 13 June 1991, p. 6
'Attali calls for the easing of EBRD restrictions on Soviet Union', 17 June 1991, p. 1
'World Bank approves new co-financing tool', 22 November 1991, p. 7
'EBRD's capital base to be doubled', 16 April 1996, p. 2
See also: 21 and 28 June, and 8 July 1994

The Times

'US hard line on aid for Russia', 16 March 1990, p. 8
'Brady attacks ambitions of EBRD', 14 April 1991, p. 1
'Attali shelves his soft loans', 14 April 1992, p. 21
'US press for change in focus at World Bank', 22 April 1991, p. 20
'Brady attacks ambitions of EBRD', 14 April 1992, p. 1

The Economist

'Growing pains at the Eurobank', 28 March 1992, pp. 107–8
'A job for Atlas and Hercules', 30 March 1991, p. 93

The Guardian

'Middle East bank key for US', 26 October 1994, p. 22
See also: 18–19 July 1994

Others

The European, 15–21 July 1994
EuroMoney, 'Plenty of money but few deals', April 1993

Index

criticisms 58–60
disagreements 48–53
and donor countries 162–6
establishment 1, 3–4, 22–3, 26–7,
    28–31, 85–6
institution building 133–41
and internationalization 112
and international relations theory
    166–8
negotiations 31–43
political mandate 179–81
and recipient countries 160–2,
    182–4
reorganization 73–6
strongest actor 71
US view 46–7
voting 27–8
European Coal and Steel Com-
    munity (ECSC) 16, 18, 154
and United States 17, 165
European Community (EC) 139
aid to CEECs 19–21, 171–2
integration theories 87
voting shares 36
see also European Union; Group
    of Twenty-Four
European Council 22–3, 26–7, 32
European Economic Community
    (EEC) 16, 154
European Investment Bank (EIB)
    27, 36
disagreement about 31–2, 48, 53
European Payments Union (EPU)
    14, 15–16, 18, 154
and Germany 17
European Recovery Plan (ERP) see
    Marshall Plan
European School for Privatization
    and Management 38

European Union 27, 85–6, 154
importance 81, 142
and Middle East 146
new members 160
see also European Community;
    European Investment Bank

Falk, Richard 99
Financial Times, The 44
first projects 76
fit 123, 141, 142
foundationalism 101, 111
France
aid to CEECs 20
Committee of European Econ-
    omic Cooperation 12
customs union 14
and ECSC 16
and EU 85–6
influence 36, 40
and Marshall Plan 13
and political aspects 41, 43
and presidency 73, 83
Frankfurt School 98, 99
Freeman, Ronald 34, 75
free trade 15, 17, 18, 38
fudging 51, 53, 134, 147

G-7 see Group of Seven
G-24 see Group of Twenty-Four
Gaddis, J. 9
Gallarotti, Giulio 135, 137–8
Galtung, John 99
game theory 63, 64–7, 72
General Agreement on Tariffs and
    Trade (GATT) 14
see also World Trade Organiz-
    ation
Georgia 76